# Driving
# Theory
## Test
# Questions
## 1999/2000

# Driving
# Theory
# Test
# Questions
## 1999/2000

### Including the questions and answers
### valid for tests taken from 2nd August 1999

Published by **BSM**
in association with
**Virgin Publishing**

First published in the UK in 1999 by
The British School of Motoring Ltd
81/87 Hartfield Road
Wimbledon
LONDON SW19 3TJ

1st reprint

ISBN 0 7535 0381 6

Cover picture and cartoons by Marc Lacey

Design, typesetting and reprographics by Prima Creative Services

Printed in Italy by arrangement with Associated Agencies Ltd

# Contents

Foreword . . . . . . . . . . . . . . . . . . . . . . . . . . . . . . . . . . . . . . . . . . . 7

Introduction . . . . . . . . . . . . . . . . . . . . . . . . . . . . . . . . . . . . . . . . . 9

**Driving Theory Test Questions**

Alertness . . . . . . . . . . . . . . . . . . . . . . . . . . . . . . . . . . . . . . . . . . . 13

Attitudes to Other Road Users . . . . . . . . . . . . . . . . . . . . . . . . . 21

Vehicle Defects, Safety Equipment and the Environment . . . . . . . . 33

Weather and Road Conditions . . . . . . . . . . . . . . . . . . . . . . . . . 47

Hazard Perception . . . . . . . . . . . . . . . . . . . . . . . . . . . . . . . . . 59

Impairment . . . . . . . . . . . . . . . . . . . . . . . . . . . . . . . . . . . . . . 73

Other Road Users . . . . . . . . . . . . . . . . . . . . . . . . . . . . . . . . . 83

Other Vehicle Characteristics . . . . . . . . . . . . . . . . . . . . . . . . . 103

Own Vehicle Handling . . . . . . . . . . . . . . . . . . . . . . . . . . . . . . 111

Roads and Regulations – Motorways . . . . . . . . . . . . . . . . . . . . 125

Roads and Regulations – Other Roads . . . . . . . . . . . . . . . . . . . 137

Signs and Signals . . . . . . . . . . . . . . . . . . . . . . . . . . . . . . . . . . 155

Documents . . . . . . . . . . . . . . . . . . . . . . . . . . . . . . . . . . . . . . 193

Accident Handling . . . . . . . . . . . . . . . . . . . . . . . . . . . . . . . . . 199

Vehicle Loading . . . . . . . . . . . . . . . . . . . . . . . . . . . . . . . . . . . 213

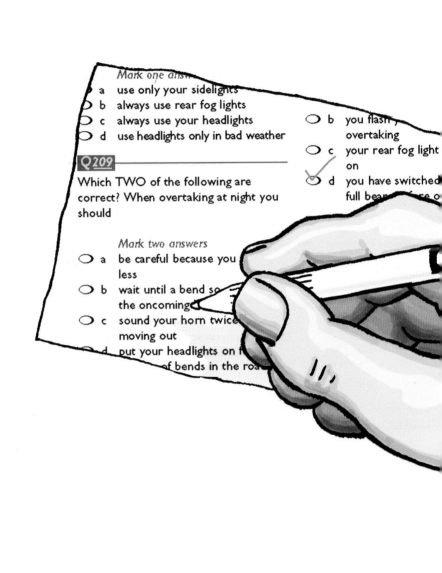

Mark one ans

a use only your sidelights
b always use rear fog lights
c always use your headlights
d use headlights only in bad weather

b you flash overtaking
c your rear fog light on
d you have switched full bea

**Q209**

Which TWO of the following are correct? When overtaking at night you should

*Mark two answers*

a be careful because you less
b wait until a bend so the oncoming
c sound your horn twice moving out
d put your headlights on of bends in the roa

# Foreword

**D**riving is an enjoyable and valuable life skill which is why every year nearly a million new learner drivers take to the road, each one of them with one clear aim. This aim is almost certainly the same as yours – to gain their full driving licence.

There is no substitute for practical experience when learning to drive. The best way to gain this is by taking lessons with a good professional driving instructor who uses the most up-to-date teaching techniques in a modern, dual-controlled car. However, it has always been equally important to prepare for your driving lessons and, since the introduction of the Theory Test, this is doubly true.

*Driving Theory Test Questions* contains the revised set (valid from 2nd August 1999) of official Driving Standards Agency questions which are currently published

and which may be included in the actual examination.

This book is an ideal study aid which allows you to test and revise your knowledge. It has been designed for use in conjunction with its companion volumes, *Pass Your Driving Theory Test* and *Pass Your Driving Test*. *Driving Theory Test Questions* allows you to check your level of knowledge by presenting you with real examination questions. The questions are set out under topic headings, and as you work through each section you will prove to yourself that you not only understand what you have learnt, but can demonstrate this by answering the question correctly.

In doing so, you will gradually boost your confidence and thereby recognise when you are ready to take and pass your Theory Test.

Your driving instructor will help you to plan your studies and ensure that you fully understand why the knowledge you acquire is essential to keep you safe on the road, as well as to take you past that first all important hurdle of passing your Theory Test.

There are no short cuts to becoming a safe and competent motorist, but that does not mean that you cannot enjoy yourself while learning.

*Driving Theory Test Questions* and its companion volumes, will, I hope, bring the Theory Test alive and make it relevant, and at the same time it should also help you develop your driving skills.

In 90 years of teaching people to drive, BSM instructors have helped millions of people pass their driving test. In my view, *Driving Theory Test Questions* completes the best set of books available to help you make the most of your driving lessons and ensure that you prepare for both the theory and practical parts of your driving test in a structured and positive way.

**Keith Cameron**
Head of Road Safety Policy

Keith Cameron is one of Britain's leading authorities on motoring and driver education. He has held a number of senior positions within the Department of Transport; including Chief Driving Examiner where he had responsibility for all UK driving tests.

# Introduction

The driving test was first introduced to the UK back in 1935. Since that time millions of people have passed the driving test and gained their motoring freedom, many taught by BSM instructors.

In 1996 a separate theory test was introduced in order to test driving knowledge and attitude. This theory test must be passed before a learner driver can apply for a practical driving test. Since its introduction the theory test has been a written paper. However, from January 2000, the theory test will be tested on computer screens.

BSM centres already offer computer based training for the theory test and can therefore help anyone who wants to prepare for their test using the latest technology. Called Theory Online, access to the BSM computers is available free to anyone taking driving lessons with BSM instructors. For details of your nearest BSM centre please call 0345 276 276.

*Driving Theory Test Questions* contains the official Driving Standards Agency questions which are currently published and which may be included in the actual examination. That means there are a lot of questions in this book (almost 900), but when you take your Theory Test, you won't be expected to answer all of them! The Test will only have 35 questions for you to answer.

I am sure your main aim is to pass the Theory Test. Nevertheless, I strongly urge to do more than simply attempt to learn the answers parrot fashion. Not only will you find such a method of learning very tedious, you will also miss out on the chance to understand the significance of the information you are learning and make use of it when you practise with your instructor.

Plus don't forget to use the BSM Theory online computers to give you the best chance of passing first time.

The list on page 11 may seem daunting, but you can be completely confident that this book and its companion volumes, *Pass Your Driving Theory Test* and *Pass Your Driving Test*, cover each of the topic areas in detail.

# Car and Motorcycle Theory Test Topics

**Before each heading below, you will see the code S1, S2, S3 or S4. This indicates in which of the four sections of this book you will find the topic covered.**

**S1 – Importance of alertness**
Concentration, anticipation, observation, awareness, distraction, boredom.

**S1 – Attitudes to other road users**
Consideration, close following, courtesy, priority.

**S1 – Knowledge of safe distances between vehicles, braking distances etc. (Conditions)**
Safety margins and effect of bad weather and road surface conditions, visibility.

**S1 – Impairment**
Knowledge of reaction times and effects on driving behaviour of alcohol, fatigue, medication, drugs, stress, ill-health, ageing, sensory impairment (including eyesight).

**S1 – Perception**
Information processing, attention, scanning, identification of hazards, time to detect hazards, fixation, interpretation.

**S1 – Judgement and decision-making**
Appropriate action, interpretation, reaction time, speed, distance.

**S2 – Risk factors associated with different road users**
Children, pedestrians, disabled people, cyclists, elderly drivers, motorcyclists, new drivers/lack of traffic experience.

**S2 – Risk factors associated with different road conditions**
Own vehicle handling. Effects of: weather, road conditions, time of day (darkness), lighting, traffic calming, speed.

**S2 – Behaviour in an accident**
Rules on how to behave in case of an accident. Use of first aid kit and other first aid precautions, setting warning device and raising alarm, police reporting procedures, witness responsibilities, regulations.

**S3 – Characteristics and statutory requirements of different types of roads**
● Limitations on motorways: speed limits, lane discipline, stopping, lighting.
● Limitations on other types of road: speed limits, parking, clearways, lighting.

**S3 – Road signs and traffic regulations**
Road traffic regulations regarding road signs, markings, signals, rights of way and speed limits.

**S4 – Administrative documents**
Rules on administrative documents required for use of vehicles.

**S4 – Safety factors relating to the vehicle and persons carried**
Vehicle loading, stability, towing, regulations.

**S4 – Mechanical aspects**
How to detect the most common mechanical faults, defects that can affect safety, understanding of implications.

**S4 – Vehicle safety equipment**
Use of safety equipment (seat belts etc).

**S4 – The environment**
Rules on vehicle use in relation to the environment, emissions, fuel consumption, pollution (including noise), regulations.

**Driving Theory Test Questions**

# Alertness

## Q001

When turning your car in the road, you should always

*Mark one answer*

- ○ a  overhang the kerb
- ○ b  use a driveway
- ● c  check all around for other road users
- ○ d  keep your hand on the handbrake

## Q002

Before you make a U-turn in the road, you should

*Mark one answer*

- ● a  give an arm signal as well as using your indicators
- ○ b  signal so that other drivers can slow down for you
- ○ c  look over your shoulder for a final check
- ○ d  select a higher gear than normal

## Q003

As a driver what does the term 'Blind Spot' mean?

*Mark one answer*

- ○ a  An area covered by your right hand mirror
- ○ b  An area not covered by your headlamps
- ○ c  An area covered by your left hand mirror
- ● d  An area not seen in your mirrors

## Q004

Objects hanging from your interior mirror may

*Mark two answers*

- ● a  restrict your view
- ○ b  improve your driving
- ● c  distract your attention
- ○ d  help your concentration

## Q005

You are most likely to lose concentration when driving if you

*Mark two answers*

- ● a  use a mobile phone
- ○ b  listen to very loud music
- ● c  switch on the heated rear window
- ○ d  look at the door mirrors

## Q006

Which FOUR are most likely to cause you to lose concentration while you are driving?

*Mark four answers*

- ● a  Using a mobile phone
- ○ b  Talking into a microphone
- ● c  Tuning your car radio
- ● d  Looking at a map
- ○ e  Checking the mirrors
- ● f  Using the demisters

**Q007**

What, according to *The Driving Manual*, do the letters MSM mean?

*Mark one answer*
- ☑ a    Mirror, signal, manoeuvre
- ○ b    Manoeuvre, signal, mirror
- ○ c    Mirror, speed, manoeuvre
- ○ d    Manoeuvre, speed, mirror

**Q008**

You are driving on a wet road. You have to stop your vehicle in an emergency. You should

*Mark one answer*
- ○ a    apply the handbrake and footbrake together
- ☑ b    keep both hands on the wheel
- ○ c    select reverse gear
- ○ d    give an arm signal

**Q009**

When following a large vehicle you should keep well back because

*Mark one answer*
- ○ a    it allows you to corner more quickly
- ○ b    it helps the large vehicle to stop more easily
- ☑ c    it allows the driver to see you in the mirrors
- ○ d    it helps you to keep out of the wind

**Q010**

As you approach this bridge you should

*Mark three answers*
- ○ a    move into the middle of the road to get a better view
- ☑ b    slow down
- ○ c    get over the bridge as quickly as possible
- ☑ d    consider using your horn
- ○ e    find another route
- ☑ f    beware of pedestrians

**Q011**

You should not use a mobile phone whilst driving

*Mark one answer*
- ○ a    until you are satisfied that no other traffic is near
- ○ b    unless you are able to drive one handed
- ☑ c    because it might distract your attention from the road ahead
- ○ d    because reception is poor when the engine is running

## Q012

In which of these situations should you avoid overtaking?

*Mark one answer*

- ○ a   Just after a bend
- ○ b   In a one-way street
- ○ c   On a 30 mph road
- ✓ d   Approaching a dip in the road

## Q013

Which of the following may cause loss of concentration on a long journey?

*Mark four answers*

- ✓ a   Loud music
- ✓ b   Arguing with a passenger
- ✓ c   Using a mobile phone
- ✓ d   Putting in a cassette tape
- ○ e   Stopping regularly to rest
- ○ f   Pulling up to tune the radio

## Q014

Your vehicle is fitted with a hands free phone system. Using this equipment whilst driving

*Mark one answer*

- ✓ a   is quite safe as long as you slow down
- ○ b   could distract your attention from the road
- ○ c   is recommended by the Highway Code
- ○ d   could be very good for road safety

## Q015

Using a hands free phone is likely to

*Mark one answer*

- ○ a   improve your safety
- ✓ b   increase your concentration
- ○ c   reduce your view
- ○ d   divert your attention

## Q016

Using a mobile phone while you are driving

*Mark one answer*

- ○ a   is acceptable in a vehicle with power steering
- ○ b   will reduce your field of vision
- ✓ c   could distract your attention from the road
- ○ d   will affect your vehicle's electronic systems

## Q017

The white arrow means that you should not plan to

*Mark one answer*

- ○ a   slow down
- ○ b   turn right
- ✓ c   overtake
- ○ d   turn left

## Q018

This road marking warns

*Mark one answer*

- ○ a drivers to use the hard shoulder
- ☑ b overtaking drivers there is a bend to the left
- ○ c overtaking drivers to move back to the left
- ○ d drivers that it is safe to overtake

## Q019

You are driving along this narrow country road. When passing the cyclist you should drive

*Mark one answer*

- ○ a slowly, sounding the horn as you pass
- ○ b quickly, leaving plenty of room
- ☑ c slowly, leaving plenty of room
- ○ d quickly, sounding the horn as you pass

## Q020

You are driving a vehicle fitted with a hand-held telephone. To use the telephone you should

*Mark one answer*

- ○ a reduce your speed
- ☑ b find a safe place to stop
- ○ c steer the vehicle with one hand
- ○ d be particularly careful at junctions

## Q021

Your mobile phone rings while you are driving on the motorway. Before answering you should

*Mark one answer*

- ○ a reduce your speed to 50 mph
- ○ b pull up on the hard shoulder
- ○ c move into the left hand lane
- ☑ d stop in a safe place

## Q022

To answer a call on your mobile phone when driving, you should

*Mark one answer*

- ○ a reduce your speed wherever you are
- ☑ b stop in a proper and convenient place
- ○ c keep the call time to a minimum
- ○ d slow down and allow others to overtake

## Q023

You want to use a mobile phone whilst driving. You should only use the phone

*Mark one answer*

- ☑ a   after stopping in a suitable place
- ◯ b   when driving on quiet, minor roads
- ◯ c   if you are driving on a motorway
- ◯ d   if you feel your driving will be unaffected

## Q024

Your mobile phone rings while you are travelling. You should

*Mark one answer*

- ◯ a   stop immediately
- ◯ b   answer it immediately
- ☑ c   pull up in a suitable place
- ◯ d   pull up at the nearest kerb

## Q025

You should ONLY use a mobile phone when

*Mark one answer*

- ◯ a   receiving a call
- ☑ b   suitably parked
- ◯ c   driving at less than 30 mph
- ◯ d   driving an automatic vehicle

## Q026

What is the safest way to use a mobile phone in your vehicle?

*Mark one answer*

- ◯ a   Use hands free equipment
- ☑ b   Find a suitable place to stop
- ◯ c   Drive slowly on a quiet road
- ◯ d   Direct your call through the operator

## Q027

Why should you be parked safely before using a mobile phone?

*Mark one answer*

- ◯ a   Because reception is better when stopped
- ☑ b   So control of your vehicle is not affected
- ◯ c   So a proper conversation can be held
- ◯ d   Because the car electrics will be affected

## Q028

On a long motorway journey boredom can cause you to feel sleepy. You should

*Mark two answers*

- ☑ a   leave the motorway and find a safe place to stop
- ◯ b   keep looking around at the surrounding landscape
- ◯ c   drive faster to complete your journey sooner
- ☑ d   ensure a supply of fresh air into your vehicle
- ◯ e   increase the volume of the car sound system
- ◯ f   stop on the hard shoulder for a rest

## Q029

You are driving at night and are dazzled by the headlights of an oncoming car. You should

*Mark one answer*

- a slow down or stop
- b close your eyes
- c flash your headlights
- ✓ d pull down the sun visor

## Q030

You are driving at dusk. You should switch your lights on

*Mark two answers*

- ✓ a even when street lights are not lit
- ✓ b so others can see you
- c only when others have done so
- d only when street lights are lit

## Q031

Why are these yellow lines painted across the road?

*Mark one answer*

- a To help you choose the correct lane
- b To help you keep the correct separation distance
- c To make you aware of your speed
- ✓ d To tell you the distance to the roundabout

## Q032

To overtake safely, which of the following applies?

*Mark one answer*

- ✓ a Check the speed and position of following traffic
- b Cut back in sharply when you have passed the vehicle
- c Get in close behind before signalling to move out
- d Steer round the vehicle sharply

## Answers and Explanations

Q001  c
Q002  c  You should always check your blind spot just before moving off or starting a manoeuvre.
Q003  d
Q004  a, c
Q005  a, b
Q006  a, b, c, d
Q007  a
Q008  b  This helps you maintain control of your car.
Q009  c
Q010  b, d, f
Q011  c
Q012  d  You cannot see if a vehicle coming towards you is hidden by the dip.
Q013  a, b, c, d
Q014  b
Q015  d  You are not allowed to use a hand-held mobile phone whilst driving. Even a hands-free

system can distract your
attention from the road.

Q016  **c**

Q017  **c**

Q018  **c**

Q019  **c**

Q020  **b** You must not use a hand-held
telephone while you are driving.

Q021  **d** If it's a hand-held phone you
must pull up before answering. If
it's hands-free it is still advisable
to stop.

Q022  **b**

Q023  **a**

Q024  **c** Answering a mobile phone
whilst driving might distract
your attention. You should
pull up first.

Q025  **b**

Q026  **b**

Q027  **b**

Q028  **a, d**

Q029  **a**

Q030  **a, b**

Q031  **c** You will need to reduce speed
on approach to the roundabout.

Q032  **a**

**Driving Theory Test Questions**

# Attitudes to Other Road Users

## Q033

A pelican crossing that crosses the road in a STRAIGHT line and has a central island MUST be treated as

*Mark one answer*
- a   one crossing in daylight only
- b   one complete crossing
- c   two separate crossings
- d   two crossings during darkness

## Q034

At a pelican crossing the flashing amber light means you should

*Mark one answer*
- a   stop and wait for the green light
- b   stop and wait for the red light
- c   give way to pedestrians waiting to cross
- d   give way to pedestrians already on the crossing

## Q035

You are approaching a pelican crossing. The amber light is flashing. You MUST

*Mark one answer*
- a   give way to pedestrians who are crossing
- b   encourage pedestrians to cross
- c   not move until the green light appears
- d   stop even if the crossing is clear

## Q036

You are driving towards a zebra crossing. Pedestrians are waiting to cross. You should

*Mark one answer*
- a   give way to the elderly and infirm only
- b   slow down and prepare to stop
- c   use your headlights to indicate they can cross
- d   wave at them to cross the road

## Q037

You have stopped at a pedestrian crossing to allow pedestrians to cross. You should

*Mark one answer*
- a   wait until they have crossed
- b   edge your vehicle forward slowly
- c   wait, revving your engine
- d   signal to pedestrians to cross

## Q038

You should never wave people across at pedestrian crossings because

*Mark one answer*
- a   there may be another vehicle coming
- b   they may not be looking
- c   it is safer for you to carry on
- d   they may not be ready to cross

**Q039**

Why should you give an arm signal on approach to a zebra crossing?

*Mark three answers*

- a  To warn following traffic
- b  To let pedestrians know you are not stopping
- c  To let pedestrians know you are slowing down
- d  To warn oncoming traffic
- e  To warn traffic you intend to turn

**Q040**

At zebra crossings you should

*Mark one answer*

- a  rev your engine to encourage pedestrians to cross quickly
- b  park only on the zig zag lines on the left
- c  always leave it clear in traffic queues
- d  wave pedestrians to cross if you intend to wait for them

**Q041**

You stop for pedestrians waiting to cross at a zebra crossing. They do not start to cross. What should you do?

*Mark one answer*

- a  Be patient and wait
- b  Sound your horn
- c  Drive on
- d  Wave them to cross

**Q042**

At puffin crossings which light will not show to a driver?

*Mark one answer*

- a  Flashing amber
- b  Red
- c  Steady amber
- d  Green

**Q043**

You are approaching a red light at a puffin crossing. Pedestrians are on the crossing. The red light will stay on until

*Mark one answer*

- a  you start to edge forward on to the crossing
- b  the pedestrians have reached a safe position
- c  the pedestrians are clear of the front of your vehicle
- d  a driver from the opposite direction reaches the crossing

**Q044**

At a puffin crossing what colour follows the green signal?

*Mark one answer*

- a  Steady red
- b  Flashing amber
- c  Steady amber
- d  Flashing green

## Q045

You could use the 'Two-Second Rule'

*Mark one answer*
- a before restarting the engine after it has stalled
- b to keep a safe gap from the vehicle in front
- c before using the 'Mirror–Signal–Manoeuvre' routine
- d when emerging on wet roads

## Q046

A two-second gap between yourself and the car in front is sufficient when conditions are

*Mark one answer*
- a wet
- b good
- c damp
- d foggy

## Q047

In fast traffic a two-second gap may be enough only when conditions are

*Mark one answer*
- a dry
- b wet
- c damp
- d foggy

## Q048

'Tailgating' means

*Mark one answer*
- a using the rear door of a hatchback car
- b reversing into a parking space
- c following another vehicle too closely
- d driving with rear fog lights on

## Q049

You are driving on a clear night. There is a steady stream of oncoming traffic. The national speed limit applies. Which lights should you use?

*Mark one answer*
- a Full beam headlights
- b Sidelights
- c Dipped headlights
- d Fog lights

## Q050

You are in a line of traffic. The driver behind you is following very closely. What action should you take?

*Mark one answer*
- a Ignore the following driver and continue to drive within the speed limit
- b Slow down, gradually increasing the gap between you and the vehicle in front
- c Signal left and wave the following driver past
- d Move over to a position just left of the centre line of the road

## Q051

Following this vehicle too closely is unwise because

*Mark one answer*
- a your brakes will overheat
- b your view ahead is increased
- c your engine will overheat
- d your view ahead is reduced

## Q052

You are following a vehicle on a wet road. You should leave a time gap of at least

*Mark one answer*
- a one second
- b two seconds
- c three seconds
- d four seconds

## Q053

You are driving behind a large goods vehicle. It signals left but steers to the right. You should

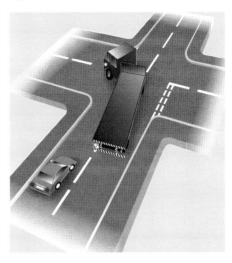

*Mark one answer*
- a slow down and let the vehicle turn
- b drive on, keeping to the left
- c overtake on the right of it
- d hold your speed and sound your horn

## Q054

You are driving at the legal speed limit. A vehicle comes up quickly behind, flashing its headlights. You should

*Mark one answer*
- a accelerate to make a gap behind you
- b touch the brakes to show your brake lights
- c maintain your speed to prevent the vehicle from overtaking
- d allow the vehicle to overtake

## Q055

You are following this lorry. You should keep well back from it to

*Mark one answer*

- a  give you a good view of the road ahead
- b  stop following traffic from rushing through the junction
- c  prevent traffic behind you from overtaking
- d  allow you to hurry through the traffic lights if they change

## Q056

You are driving in traffic at the speed limit for the road. The driver behind is trying to overtake. You should

*Mark one answer*

- a  move closer to the car ahead, so the driver behind has no room to overtake
- b  wave the driver behind to overtake when it is safe
- c  keep a steady course and allow the driver behind to overtake
- d  accelerate to get away from the driver behind

## Q057

You are driving along this road. The red van cuts in close in front of you. What should you do?

*Mark one answer*

- a  Accelerate to get closer to the red van
- b  Give a long blast on the horn
- c  Drop back to leave the correct separation distance
- d  Flash your headlights several times

## Q058

You are waiting in a traffic queue at night. To avoid dazzling following drivers you should

*Mark one answer*

- a  apply the handbrake only
- b  apply the footbrake only
- c  switch off your headlights
- d  use both the handbrake and footbrake

**Q059**

When are you allowed to exceed the maximum speed limit?

*Mark one answer*
- a  Between midnight and 6 am
- b  At no time
- c  When overtaking
- d  When the road is clear

**Q060**

You are driving at the legal speed limit. A vehicle behind wants to overtake. Should you try to prevent the driver overtaking?

*Mark one answer*
- a  No, unless it is safe to do so
- b  Yes, because the other driver is acting dangerously
- c  No, not at any time
- d  Yes, because the other driver is breaking the law

**Q061**

You are driving at night on an unlit road following a slower moving vehicle. You should

*Mark one answer*
- a  flash your headlights
- b  use dipped beam headlights
- c  switch off your headlights
- d  use full beam headlights

**Q062**

A long, heavily-laden lorry is taking a long time to overtake you. What should you do?

*Mark one answer*
- a  Speed up
- b  Slow down
- c  Hold your speed
- d  Change direction

**Q063**

You are driving a slow-moving vehicle on a narrow, winding road. You should

*Mark one answer*
- a  keep well out to stop vehicles overtaking dangerously
- b  wave following vehicles past you if you think they can overtake quickly
- c  pull in safely when you can, to let following vehicles overtake
- d  give a left signal when it is safe for vehicles to overtake you

**Q064**

You are driving a slow-moving vehicle on a narrow road. When traffic wishes to overtake you should

*Mark one answer*
- a  take no action
- b  put your hazard warning lights on
- c  stop immediately and wave it on
- d  pull in safely as soon as you can do so

## Q065

You are driving a slow-moving vehicle on a narrow, winding road. In order to let other vehicles overtake you should

*Mark one answer*
- a  wave to them to pass
- b  pull in when you can
- c  show a left turn signal
- d  keep left and hold your speed

## Q066

Which of the following vehicles will use blue flashing beacons?

*Mark three answers*
- a  Motorway maintenance
- b  Bomb disposal
- c  Blood transfusion
- d  Police patrol
- e  Breakdown recovery

## Q067

Which THREE of these emergency services might have blue flashing beacons?

*Mark three answers*
- a  Coastguard
- b  Bomb disposal
- c  Gritting lorries
- d  Animal ambulances
- e  Mountain rescue
- f  Doctors' cars

## Q068

When being followed by an ambulance showing a flashing blue beacon you should

*Mark one answer*
- a  pull over as soon as safely possible to let it pass
- b  accelerate hard to get away from it
- c  maintain your speed and course
- d  brake harshly and immediately stop in the road

## Q069

You see a car showing a flashing green beacon. Should you give way to it?

*Mark one answer*
- a  Yes, it is a doctor going to an emergency
- b  Yes, it is a fire crew support vehicle
- c  No, it is a slow moving vehicle
- d  No, it is a breakdown vehicle

## Q070

What type of emergency vehicle is fitted with a green flashing beacon?

*Mark one answer*
- a  Fire engine
- b  Road gritter
- c  Ambulance
- d  Doctor's car

**Q071**

A flashing green beacon on a vehicle means

*Mark one answer*
- a police on non-urgent duties
- b doctor on an emergency call
- c road safety patrol operating
- d gritting in progress

**Q072**

A vehicle has a flashing green beacon. What does this mean?

*Mark one answer*
- a A doctor is answering an emergency call
- b The vehicle is slow-moving
- c It is a motorway police patrol vehicle
- d A vehicle is carrying hazardous chemicals

**Q073**

Diamond-shaped signs give instructions to

*Mark one answer*
- a tram drivers
- b bus drivers
- c lorry drivers
- d taxi drivers

**Q074**

On a road where trams operate, which of these vehicles will be most at risk from the tram rails?

*Mark one answer*
- a Cars
- b Cycles
- c Buses
- d Lorries

**Q075**

At unmarked junctions where tram lines cross over roads, who has priority?

*Mark one answer*
- a Cars
- b Motorcycles
- c Trams
- d Buses

**Q076**

You should ONLY flash your headlights to other road users

*Mark one answer*
- a to show that you are giving way
- b to show that you are about to reverse
- c to tell them that you have right of way
- d to let them know that you are there

## Q077

A bus is stopped at a bus stop ahead of you. Its right-hand indicator is flashing. You should

*Mark one answer*

- a   flash your headlights and slow down
- b   slow down and give way if it is safe to do so
- c   sound your horn and keep going
- d   slow down and then sound your horn

## Q078

A bus lane on your left shows no times of operation. This means it is

*Mark one answer*

- a   not in operation at all
- b   only in operation at peak times
- c   in operation 24 hours a day
- d   only in operation in daylight hours

## Q079

What should you use your horn for?

*Mark one answer*

- a   To alert others to your presence
- b   To allow you right of way
- c   To greet other road users
- d   To signal your annoyance

## Q080

A vehicle pulls out in front of you at a junction. What should you do?

*Mark one answer*

- a   Swerve past it and blow your horn
- b   Flash your headlights and drive up close behind
- c   Slow down and be ready to stop
- d   Accelerate past it immediately

## Q081

You are in a one-way street and want to turn right. You should position yourself

*Mark one answer*

- a   in the right-hand lane
- b   in the left-hand lane
- c   in either lane, depending on the traffic
- d   just left of the centre line

## Q082

When overtaking a horse and rider you should

*Mark one answer*

- a   sound your horn as a warning
- b   go past as quickly as possible
- c   flash your headlights as a warning
- d   go past slowly and carefully

**Q083**

You wish to turn right ahead. Why should you take up the correct position in good time?

*Mark one answer*
- a To allow other drivers to pull out in front of you
- b To give a better view into the road that you're joining
- c To help other road users know what you intend to do
- d To allow drivers to pass you on the right

**Q084**

You are driving along a country road. A horse and rider are approaching. What should you do?

*Mark two answers*
- a Increase your speed
- b Sound your horn
- c Flash your headlights
- d Drive slowly past
- e Give plenty of room
- f Rev your engine

**Q085**

A person herding sheep asks you to stop. You should

*Mark one answer*
- a ignore them as they have no authority
- b stop and switch off your engine
- c continue on but drive slowly
- d try and get past quickly

**Q086**

Which of the following are at greatest risk from other road users?

*Mark one answer*
- a Motorcyclists
- b Lorry drivers
- c Learner car drivers
- d Busy bus drivers

## Answers and Explanations

Q033 b
Q034 d
Q035 a You must give way to pedestrians already on the crossing but may drive on if the crossing is clear.
Q036 b
Q037 a
Q038 a
Q039 a, c, d
Q040 c
Q041 a Pedestrians are naturally nervous and cautious at crossings, so allow them time. Only drive on if you are certain they do not intend to cross.
Q042 a
Q043 b
Q044 c
Q045 b A two-second time gap from the vehicle in front provides a safe gap in good conditions.
Q046 b
Q047 a
Q048 c

Q049 c

Q050 b By increasing the gap between you and the vehicle in front, you give yourself and the driver behind more room to stop should you need it.

Q051 d If you hang back you will have a much better view of the road ahead.

Q052 d In good conditions you should allow two seconds but on a wet road you double this to four.

Q053 a

Q054 d This is your only safe option.

Q055 a The nearer you are to a lorry, the less you can see ahead.

Q056 c

Q057 c

Q058 a Using the footbrake would activate your brake lights and might dazzle following drivers.

Q059 b

Q060 c Even if other drivers are breaking the law or acting dangerously, you are likely to increase the danger if you try to prevent them overtaking.

Q061 b

Q062 b By slowing down you allow the lorry to get past, which is the only safe option.

Q063 c 'a' and 'b' are dangerous and 'd' is confusing. Other drivers might think you are stopping or turning left.

Q064 d

Q065 b

Q066 b, c, d

Q067 a, b, e

Q068 a

Q069 a

Q070 d Doctors on emergency call may display a flashing green beacon. Slow-moving vehicles have amber flashing beacons. Police, fire and ambulance service vehicles have blue flashing beacons.

Q071 b

Q072 a

Q073 a

Q074 b

Q075 c

Q076 d You should only flash your headlights to warn other road users that you are there.

Q077 b

Q078 c

Q079 a

Q080 c This is the only safe thing to do. The other answers are the actions of an aggressive driver.

Q081 a To turn right from a one-way street you normally position yourself in the right-hand lane.

Q082 d

Q083 c The position of your car helps signal your intentions to other drivers.

Q084 d, e

Q085 b

Q086 a

**Driving Theory Test Questions**

# Vehicle Defects, Safety Equipment and the Environment

## Q087

When should you especially check the engine oil level?

*Mark one answer*

- a   Before a long journey
- b   When the engine is hot
- c   Early in the morning
- d   Every 6000 miles

## Q088

Which of these, if allowed to get low, could cause an accident?

*Mark one answer*

- a   Antifreeze level
- b   Brake fluid level
- c   Battery water level
- d   Radiator coolant level

## Q089

Which TWO are badly affected if the tyres are under-inflated?

*Mark two answers*

- a   Braking
- b   Steering
- c   Changing gear
- d   Parking

## Q090

It is important that tyre pressures are correct. They should be checked at least

*Mark one answer*

- a   every time the vehicle is serviced
- b   once a week
- c   once a month
- d   every time the vehicle has an MOT test

## Q091

What can cause heavy steering?

*Mark one answer*

- a   Driving on ice
- b   Badly worn brakes
- c   Over-inflated tyres
- d   Under-inflated tyres

## Q092

Which THREE does the law require you to keep in good condition?

*Mark three answers*

- a   Gears
- b   Transmission
- c   Headlights
- d   Windscreen
- e   Seat belts

## Q093

Your car is fitted with power assisted steering. This will make the steering seem

*Mark one answer*

- a   lighter
- b   heavier
- c   quieter
- d   noisier

## Q094

Which FOUR of these MUST be in good working order for your car to be roadworthy?

*Mark four answers*

- a   Temperature gauge
- b   Speedometer
- c   Windscreen washers
- d   Windscreen wipers
- e   Oil warning light
- f   Horn

## Q095

It is essential that tyre pressures are checked regularly. When should this be done?

*Mark one answer*
- a   After any lengthy journey
- b   After driving at high speed
- c   When tyres are hot
- d   When tyres are cold

## Q096

Driving with under-inflated tyres can affect

*Mark two answers*
- a   engine temperature
- b   fuel consumption
- c   braking
- d   oil pressure

## Q097

A police officer orders you to stop. He finds you have a faulty tyre. Who is responsible for the tyre?

*Mark one answer*
- a   The previous owner
- b   Whoever services the car
- c   You, the driver
- d   Whoever issued the MOT certificate

## Q098

It is illegal to drive with tyres that

*Mark one answer*
- a   have been bought second-hand
- b   have a large deep cut in the side wall
- c   are of different makes
- d   are of different tread patterns

## Q099

The legal minimum depth of tread for car tyres over three quarters of the breadth is

*Mark one answer*
- a   1 mm
- b   1.6 mm
- c   2.5 mm
- d   4 mm

## Q100

Excessive or uneven tyre wear can be caused by faults in the

*Mark two answers*
- a   gearbox
- b   braking system
- c   suspension
- d   exhaust system

## Q101

There is vibration on your steering wheel as you drive. You should check that the

*Mark one answer*
- a   doors are closed
- b   wheels are balanced
- c   exhaust is not loose
- d   engine oil level is correct

## Q102

Your vehicle pulls to one side when braking. You should

*Mark one answer*
- a   change the tyres around
- b   consult your garage as soon as possible
- c   pump the pedal when braking
- d   use your handbrake at the same time

## Q103

The main cause of brake fade is

*Mark one answer*
- a   the brakes overheating
- b   air in the brake fluid
- c   oil on the brakes
- d   the brakes out of adjustment

## Q104

New petrol-engined cars must be fitted with catalytic converters. The reason for this is to

*Mark one answer*
- a   control exhaust noise levels
- b   prolong the life of the exhaust system
- c   allow the exhaust system to be recycled
- d   reduce harmful exhaust emissions

## Q105

Waste engine oil should be disposed of

*Mark one answer*
- a   at the local demolition site
- b   down a water drain
- c   at the local authority site
- d   on nearby waste land

## Q106

If you notice a strong smell of petrol as you drive along you should

*Mark one answer*
- a   not worry, as it is only exhaust fumes
- b   carry on at a reduced speed
- c   expect it to stop in a few miles
- d   stop and investigate the problem

## Q107

You are driving on a motorway. The traffic ahead is braking sharply because of an accident. How could you warn following traffic?

*Mark one answer*
- a   Briefly use the hazard warning lights
- b   Switch on the hazard warning lights continuously
- c   Briefly use the rear fog lights
- d   Switch on the headlamps continuously

## Q108

Your anti-lock brakes warning light stays on. You should

*Mark one answer*
- a   check the brake fluid level
- b   check the footbrake free play
- c   check that the handbrake is released
- d   have the brakes checked immediately

## Q109

What does this instrument panel light mean when lit ?

*Mark one answer*
- a   Gear lever in park
- b   Gear lever in neutral
- c   Handbrake on
- d   Handbrake off

**Q110**

When MUST you use dipped headlights during the day?

*Mark one answer*

○ a  All the time
○ b  Along narrow streets
○ c  In poor visibility
○ d  When parking

**Q111**

Which instrument panel warning light would show that headlamps are on full beam ?

*Mark one answer*

 ○ a

 ○ b

 ○ c

 ○ d

**Q112**

While driving, this warning light on your dashboard comes on. It means

*Mark one answer*

○ a  a fault in the braking system
○ b  the engine oil is low
○ c  a rear light has failed
○ d  your seat belt is not fastened

**Q113**

When may you use hazard warning lights?

*Mark one answer*

○ a  To park alongside another car
○ b  To park on double yellow lines
○ c  When you are being towed
○ d  When you have broken down

**Q114**

Hazard warning lights should be used when vehicles are

*Mark one answer*

○ a  broken down and causing an obstruction
○ b  faulty and moving slowly
○ c  being towed along a road
○ d  reversing into a side road

**Q115**

It is important to wear suitable shoes when you are driving. Why is this?

*Mark one answer*

○ a  To prevent wear on the pedals
○ b  To maintain control of the pedals
○ c  To enable you to adjust your seat
○ d  To enable you to walk for assistance if you break down

**Q116**

A properly adjusted head restraint will

*Mark one answer*

○ a  make you more comfortable
○ b  help you to avoid neck injury
○ c  help you to relax
○ d  help you to maintain your driving position

## Q117

What will reduce the risk of neck injury resulting from a collision?

*Mark one answer*
- a   An air-sprung seat
- b   Anti-lock brakes
- c   A collapsible steering wheel
- d   A properly adjusted head restraint

## Q118

How can you, as a driver, help the environment?

*Mark three answers*
- a   By reducing your speed
- b   By gentle acceleration
- c   By using leaded fuel
- d   By driving faster
- e   By harsh acceleration
- f   By servicing your vehicle properly

## Q119

To help the environment, you can avoid wasting fuel by

*Mark three answers*
- a   having your vehicle properly serviced
- b   making sure your tyres are correctly inflated
- c   not over-revving in the lower gears
- d   driving at higher speeds where possible
- e   keeping an empty roof rack properly fitted
- f   servicing your vehicle less regularly

## Q120

Which THREE things can you, as a road user, do to help the environment?

*Mark three answers*
- a   Cycle when possible
- b   Drive on under-inflated tyres
- c   Use the choke for as long as possible on a cold engine
- d   Have your vehicle properly tuned and serviced
- e   Watch the traffic and plan ahead
- f   Brake as late as possible without skidding

## Q121

Why do MOT tests include a strict exhaust emission test?

*Mark one answer*
- a   To recover the cost of expensive garage equipment
- b   To help protect the environment against pollution
- c   To discover which fuel supplier is used the most
- d   To make sure diesel and petrol engines emit the same fumes

## Q122

As a driver you can cause MORE damage to the environment by

*Mark three answers*
- a   choosing a fuel efficient vehicle
- b   making a lot of short journeys
- c   driving in as high a gear as possible
- d   accelerating as quickly as possible
- e   having your vehicle regularly serviced
- f   using leaded fuel

**Q123**

You are driving a friend's children home from school. They are both under 14 years old. Who is responsible for making sure they wear a seat belt?

*Mark one answer*

○ a   An adult passenger
○ b   The children
○ c   You, the driver
○ d   Your friend

**Q124**

Motor vehicles can harm the environment. This has resulted in

*Mark three answers*

○ a   air pollution
○ b   damage to buildings
○ c   reduced health risks
○ d   improved public transport
○ e   less use of electrical vehicles
○ f   using up natural resources

**Q125**

To help protect the environment you should NOT

*Mark one answer*

○ a   remove your roof rack when unloaded
○ b   use your car for very short journeys
○ c   walk, cycle, or use public transport
○ d   empty the boot of unnecessary weight

**Q126**

You service your own vehicle. How should you get rid of the old engine oil?

*Mark one answer*

○ a   Take it to a local authority site
○ b   Pour it down a drain
○ c   Tip it into a hole in the ground
○ d   Put it into your dustbin

**Q127**

To reduce the damage your vehicle causes to the environment you should

*Mark three answers*

○ a   use narrow side streets
○ b   avoid harsh acceleration
○ c   brake in good time
○ d   anticipate well ahead
○ e   use busy routes

**Q128**

You will help the environment if you

*Mark one answer*

○ a   reduce the tyre pressures
○ b   drive continually using full choke
○ c   accelerate and brake sharply
○ d   walk or cycle when you can

**Q129**

You are carrying two 13 year old children and their parents in your car. Who is responsible for seeing that the children wear seat belts?

*Mark one answer*

○ a   The children's parents
○ b   You, the driver
○ c   The front-seat passenger
○ d   The children

## Q130

Car passengers MUST wear a seat belt if one is available, unless they are

*Mark one answer*
- a under 14 years old
- b under 1.5 metres (5 feet) in height
- c sitting in the rear seat
- d exempt for medical reasons

## Q131

Extra care should be taken when refuelling, because diesel fuel when spilt is

*Mark one answer*
- a sticky
- b odourless
- c clear
- d slippery

## Q132

Excessive or uneven tyre wear can be caused by faults in which THREE?

*Mark three answers*
- a The gearbox
- b The braking system
- c The accelerator
- d The exhaust system
- e Wheel alignment
- f The suspension

## Q133

What will cause high fuel consumption?

*Mark one answer*
- a Poor steering control
- b Accelerating around bends
- c Driving in high gears
- d Harsh braking and accelerating

## Q134

You must NOT sound your horn

*Mark one answer*
- a between 10 pm and 6 am in a built-up area
- b at any time in a built-up area
- c between 11.30 pm and 7 am in a built-up area
- d between 11.30 pm and 6 am on any road

## Q135

You are testing your suspension. You notice that your vehicle keeps bouncing when you press down on the front wing. What does this mean?

*Mark one answer*
- a Worn tyres
- b Tyres under-inflated
- c Steering wheel not located centrally
- d Worn shock absorbers

## Q136

You have a loose filler cap on your diesel fuel tank. This will

*Mark two answers*
- a waste fuel and money
- b make roads slippery for other road users
- c improve your vehicles fuel consumption
- d increase the level of exhaust emissions

## Q137

Which of the following will improve fuel consumption?

*Mark two answers*
- a Reducing your road speed
- b Planning well ahead
- c Late and harsh braking
- d Driving in lower gears
- e Short journeys with a cold engine
- f Rapid acceleration

## Q138

Which THREE of the following are most likely to waste fuel?

*Mark three answers*
- a Reducing your speed
- b Carrying unnecessary weight
- c Using the wrong grade of fuel
- d Under-inflated tyres
- e Using different brands of fuel
- f A fitted, empty roof rack

## Q139

In which of these containers may you carry petrol in a motor vehicle?

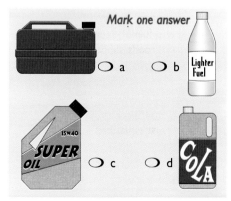

*Mark one answer*
- a
- b Lighter Fuel
- c SUPER OIL 15W40
- d COLA

## Q140

To avoid spillage after refuelling, you should make sure that

*Mark one answer*
- a your tank is only 3/4 full
- b you have used a locking filler cap
- c you check your fuel gauge is working
- d your filler cap is securely fastened

## Q141

When should you NOT use your horn in a built-up area?

*Mark one answer*
- a Between 8 pm and 8 am
- b Between 9 pm and dawn
- c Between dusk and 8 am
- d Between 11.30 pm and 7 am

## Q142

Why are mirrors on the outside of vehicles often slightly curved (convex)?

*Mark one answer*
- a They give a wider field of vision
- b They totally cover blind spots
- c They make it easier to judge the speed of following traffic
- d They make following traffic look bigger

## Q143

A properly serviced vehicle will give

*Mark two answers*
- a lower insurance premiums
- b you a refund on your road tax
- c better fuel economy
- d cleaner exhaust emissions

## Q144

You cannot see clearly behind when reversing. What should you do?

*Mark one answer*

- a  Open your window to look behind
- b  Open the door and look behind
- c  Look in the nearside mirror
- d  Ask someone to guide you

## Q145

Driving at 70 mph uses more fuel than driving at 50 mph by up to

*Mark one answer*

- a  10%
- b  30%
- c  75%
- d  100%

## Q146

When driving a car fitted with automatic transmission what would you use 'kick down' for?

*Mark one answer*

- a  Cruise control
- b  Quick acceleration
- c  Slow braking
- d  Fuel economy

## Q147

When a roof rack is not in use it should be removed. Why is this?

*Mark one answer*

- a  It will affect the suspension
- b  It is illegal
- c  It will affect your braking
- d  It will waste fuel

## Q148

A roof rack fitted to your car will

*Mark one answer*

- a  reduce fuel consumption
- b  improve the road handling
- c  make your car go faster
- d  increase fuel consumption

## Q149

The pictured vehicle is 'environmentally friendly' because it

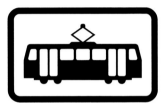

*Mark three answers*

- a  reduces noise pollution
- b  uses diesel fuel
- c  uses electricity
- d  uses unleaded fuel
- e  reduces parking spaces
- f  reduces town traffic

## Q150

Supertrams or Light Rapid Transit (LRT) systems are environmentally friendly because

*Mark one answer*

- a  they use diesel power
- b  they use quieter roads
- c  they use electric power
- d  they do not operate during rush hour

**Q151**

'Red routes' in major cities have been introduced to

*Mark one answer*
- a  raise the speed limits
- b  help the traffic flow
- c  provide better parking
- d  allow lorries to load more freely

**Q152**

To reduce the volume of traffic on the roads you could

*Mark three answers*
- a  use public transport more often
- b  share a car when possible
- c  walk or cycle on short journeys
- d  travel by car at all times
- e  use a car with a smaller engine
- f  drive in a bus lane

**Q153**

In some narrow residential streets you will find a speed limit of

*Mark one answer*
- a  20 mph
- b  25 mph
- c  35 mph
- d  40 mph

**Q154**

Road humps, chicanes, and narrowings are

*Mark one answer*
- a  always at major road works
- b  used to increase traffic speed
- c  at toll-bridge approaches only
- d  traffic calming measures

**Q155**

You enter a road where there are road humps. What should you do?

*Mark one answer*
- a  Maintain a reduced speed throughout
- b  Accelerate quickly between each one
- c  Always keep to the maximum legal speed
- d  Drive slowly at school times only

**Q156**

On your vehicle, where would you find a catalytic converter?

*Mark one answer*
- a  In the fuel tank
- b  In the air filter
- c  On the cooling system
- d  On the exhaust system

**Q157**

Leaded petrol must NOT be used in vehicles fitted with

*Mark one answer*
- a  a fuel injection system
- b  a catalytic converter
- c  an engine of less than 1000 cc
- d  a stainless steel exhaust

## Q158

New vehicles are fitted with catalytic converters if they use

*Mark one answer*
- a   gas power
- b   unleaded petrol
- c   leaded petrol
- d   battery power

## Q159

For which TWO of these may you use hazard warning lights?

*Mark two answers*
- a   When driving on a motorway, to warn other drivers behind of a hazard ahead
- b   When you are double parked on a two-way road
- c   When your direction indicators are not working
- d   When warning oncoming traffic that you intend to stop
- e   When your vehicle has broken down and is causing an obstruction

## Q160

Daytime visibility is poor but not seriously reduced. You should switch on

*Mark one answer*
- a   headlights and fog lights
- b   front fog lights
- c   dipped headlights
- d   rear fog lights

## Q161

Why are vehicles fitted with rear fog lights?

*Mark one answer*
- a   To be seen when driving at high speed
- b   To use if broken down in a dangerous position
- c   To make them more visible in thick fog
- d   To warn drivers following closely to drop back

### Answers and Explanations

Q087   a
Q088   b   A low level of brake fluid may cause your brakes to fail.
Q089   a, b
Q090   b   Incorrect tyre pressures can affect the control and road holding of the vehicle and lead to excessive tyre wear.
Q091   d
Q092   c, d, e
Q093   a
Q094   b, c, d, f   These must, by law, be in good working order.
Q095   d
Q096   b, c
Q097   c
Q098   b
Q099   b
Q100   b, c
Q101   b
Q102   b
Q103   a

Q104   d   This helps the car operate more efficiently and cause less air pollution. Only unleaded fuel may be used.

Q105   c   Waste engine oil is harmful to the environment. It will be disposed of safely at a local authority site.

Q106   d   Your car might catch fire if you drove on.

Q107   a

Q108   d

Q109   c

Q110   c

Q111   a

Q112   a

Q113   d   You should not use hazard warning lights when being towed so 'c' is wrong.

Q114   a

Q115   b

Q116   b

Q117   d   If you are involved in an accident, the head restraint helps protect your neck from whiplash.

Q118   a, b, f

Q119   a, b, c

Q120   a, d, e

Q121   b

Q122   b, d, f   A lot of short journeys use up a lot of petrol and pollute the atmosphere with the exhaust fumes.

Q123   c

Q124   a, b, f

Q125   b

Q126   a

Q127   b, c, d   Doing these make for smoother driving which uses less fuel and so cuts down on pollution.

Q128   d

Q129   b

Q130   d   All passengers, front and rear, must wear seat belts, if fitted, unless exempt for medical reasons.

Q131   d

Q132   b, e, f

Q133   d   Harsh braking is one of the major causes of high fuel consumption.

Q134   c   The regulation only applies in a built up area.

Q135   d

Q136   a, b

Q137   a, b

Q138   b, d, f

Q139   a

Q140   d

Q141   d

Q142   a   Convex mirrors give a wider field of vision but also make traffic look further away than it really is, so you need to use them with care.

Q143   c, d

Q144   d   If you cannot see properly you need to get someone to help.

Q145   b

Q146   b   A short, firm pressure right down on the gas pedal causes a quick change down to the next lower gear – useful, for example, when you need to overtake.

Q147   d

Q148   d

Q149   a, c, f

Q150   c

Q151   b

Q152   a, b, c

Q153  **a**  This is a traffic calming measure.

Q154  **d**

Q155  **a**  Road humps are there to slow the traffic in residential areas.

Q156  **d**

Q157  **b**  Only unleaded petrol can be used in vehicles fitted with a catalytic converter.

Q158  **b**

Q159  **a, e**

Q160  **c**

Q161  **c**  If visibility drops below about 100 metres (328 feet) use fog lights.

**Driving Theory Test Questions**

# Weather and Road Conditions

## Q162

Your vehicle is fitted with anti-lock brakes. To stop quickly in an emergency you should

*Mark one answer*
- ○ a brake firmly and pump the brake pedal on and off
- ⊘ b brake rapidly and firmly without releasing the brake pedal
- ○ c brake gently and pump the brake pedal on and off
- ○ d brake rapidly once, and immediately release the brake pedal

## Q163

Anti-lock brakes reduce the chances of a skid occurring particularly when

*Mark one answer*
- ○ a driving down steep hills
- ○ b braking during normal driving
- ⊘ c braking in an emergency
- ○ d driving on good road surfaces

## Q164

Your car is fitted with anti-lock brakes. You need to stop in an emergency. You should

*Mark one answer*
- ⊘ a brake normally and avoid turning the steering wheel
- ○ b press the brake pedal rapidly and firmly until you have stopped
- ○ c keep pushing and releasing the foot brake quickly to prevent skidding
- ○ d apply the handbrake to reduce the stopping distance

## Q165

You are driving a vehicle fitted with anti-lock brakes. You need to stop in an emergency. You should apply the footbrake

*Mark one answer*
- ○ a slowly and gently
- ⊘ b slowly but firmly ✗
- ○ c rapidly and gently
- ○ d rapidly and firmly

## Q166

Vehicles fitted with anti-lock brakes

*Mark one answer*
- ○ a are impossible to skid
- ⊘ b can be steered while you are braking
- ○ c accelerate much faster
- ○ d are not fitted with a handbrake

## Q167

Anti-lock brakes may not work as effectively if the road surface is

*Mark two answers*
- ○ a dry
- ⊘ b loose
- ⊘ c wet
- ○ d good
- ○ e firm

## Q168

Anti-lock brakes are of most use when you are

*Mark one answer*
- ⊘ a braking gently
- ○ b driving on worn tyres
- ○ c braking excessively
- ○ d driving normally

## Q169

When would an anti-lock braking system start to work?

*Mark one answer*

- a After the parking brake has been applied
- b Whenever pressure on the brake pedal is applied
- c Just as the wheels are about to lock ①
- d When the normal braking system fails to operate

## Q170

Your vehicle has anti-lock brakes, but they may not always prevent skidding. This is most likely to happen when driving

*Mark two answers*

- a in foggy conditions ①
- b on surface water
- c on loose road surfaces
- d on dry tarmac
- e at night on unlit roads

## Q171

Anti-lock brakes are most effective when you ①

*Mark one answer*

- a keep pumping the foot brake to prevent skidding
- b brake normally, but grip the steering wheel tightly
- c brake rapidly and firmly until you have slowed down
- d apply the handbrake to reduce the stopping distance

## Q172

Anti-lock brakes will take effect when

*Mark one answer*

- a you do not brake quickly enough
- b excessive brake pressure has been applied
- c you have not seen a hazard ahead
- d speeding on slippery road surfaces

## Q173

Anti-lock brakes can greatly assist with

*Mark one answer*

- a a higher cruising speed
- b steering control when braking
- c control when accelerating
- d motorway driving

## Q174

You are on a good, dry road surface and your vehicle has good brakes and tyres. What is the overall stopping distance at 40 mph?

*Mark one answer*

- a 23 metres (75 feet)
- b 36 metres (118 feet)
- c 53 metres (174 feet)
- d 96 metres (315 feet)

## Q175

You are on a good, dry road surface. Your vehicle has good brakes and tyres. What is the braking distance at 50 mph?

*Mark one answer*

- a 38 metres (125 feet)
- b 14 metres (46 feet)
- c 24 metres (79 feet)
- d 55 metres (180 feet)

## Q176

Braking hard at speed on a sharp bend can make your vehicle

*Mark one answer*
- a  more stable
- b  unstable
- c  stall
- d  corner safely

## Q177

What is the shortest stopping distance at 70 mph?

*Mark one answer*
- a  53 metres (174 feet)
- b  60 metres (197 feet)
- c  73 metres (240 feet)
- d  96 metres (315 feet)

## Q178

Anti-lock brakes prevent wheels from locking. This means the tyres are less likely to

*Mark one answer*
- a  aquaplane
- b  skid
- c  puncture
- d  wear

## Q179

What is the shortest overall stopping distance on a dry road from 60 mph?

*Mark one answer*
- a  53 metres (174 feet)
- b  58 metres (190 feet)
- c  73 metres (240 feet)
- d  96 metres (315 feet)

## Q180

When driving in fog, which of the following are correct?

*Mark three answers*
- a  Use dipped headlights
- b  Use headlights on full beam
- c  Allow more time for your journey
- d  Keep close to the car in front
- e  Slow down
- f  Use side lights only

## Q181

You are on a fast, open road in good conditions. For safety, the distance between you and the vehicle in front should be

*Mark one answer*
- a  a two-second time gap
- b  one car length
- c  2 metres (6 feet 6 inches)
- d  two car lengths

## Q182

The 'Two-Second Rule' helps you to

*Mark one answer*
- a  keep a safe distance from the car in front
- b  keep the correct distance from the kerb
- c  check your blind spot
- d  check your mirrors

**Q183**

Driving a vehicle fitted with anti-lock brakes allows you to

*Mark one answer*

- a brake harder because it is impossible to skid
- b drive at higher speeds
- c steer and brake at the same time
- d pay less attention to the road ahead

**Q184**

What is the main reason why your stopping distance is longer after heavy rain?

*Mark one answer*

- a You may not be able to see large puddles
- b The brakes will be cold because they are wet
- c Your tyres will have less grip on the road
- d Water on the windscreen will blur your view of the road ahead

**Q185**

You are travelling at 50 mph on a good, dry road. What is your shortest overall stopping distance?

*Mark one answer*

- a 36 metres (118 feet)
- b 53 metres (174 feet)
- c 75 metres (245 feet)
- d 96 metres (315 feet)

**Q186**

What is the most common cause of skidding?

*Mark one answer*

- a Worn tyres
- b Driver error
- c Other vehicles
- d Pedestrians

**Q187**

When braking hard in a straight line, the weight of the vehicle will shift onto the

*Mark one answer*

- a front wheels
- b rear wheels
- c left wheels
- d right wheels

**Q188**

You are driving in heavy rain. Your steering suddenly becomes very light. You should

*Mark one answer*

- a steer towards the side of the road
- b apply gentle acceleration
- c brake firmly to reduce speed
- d ease off the accelerator

**Q189**

You have driven through a flood. What is the first thing you should do?

*Mark one answer*

- a Stop and check the tyres
- b Stop and dry the brakes
- c Switch on your windscreen wipers
- d Test your brakes

**Q190**

You are driving along a country road. You see this sign. AFTER dealing safely with the hazard you should always

*Mark one answer*
- a check your tyre pressures
- b switch on your hazard warning lights
- c accelerate briskly
- d test your brakes

**Q191**

Braking distances on ice can be

*Mark one answer*
- a twice the normal distance
- b five times the normal distance
- c seven times the normal distance
- d ten times the normal distance

**Q192**

Freezing conditions will affect the distance it takes you to come to a stop. You should expect stopping distances to increase by up to

*Mark one answer*
- a two times
- b five times
- c three times
- d ten times

**Q193**

When driving in icy conditions, the steering becomes light because the tyres

*Mark one answer*
- a have more grip on the road
- b are too soft
- c are too hard
- d have less grip on the road

**Q194**

You are driving on an icy road. How can you avoid wheelspin?

*Mark one answer*
- a Drive at a slow speed in as high a gear as possible
- b Use the handbrake if the wheels start to slip
- c Brake gently and repeatedly
- d Drive in a low gear at all times

**Q195**

Your overall stopping distance will be much longer when driving

*Mark one answer*
- a in the rain
- b in fog
- c at night
- d in strong winds

**Q196**

Skidding is mainly caused by

*Mark one answer*
- a the weather
- b the driver
- c the vehicle
- d the road

## Q197

How can you avoid wheelspin when driving in freezing conditions?

*Mark one answer*

- ○ a  Stay in first gear all the time
- ○ b  Put on your handbrake if the wheels begin to slip
- ○ c  Drive in as high a gear as possible
- ○ d  Allow the vehicle to coast in neutral

## Q198

You are driving in freezing conditions. What should you do when approaching a sharp bend?

*Mark two answers*

- ○ a  Slow down before you reach the bend
- ○ b  Gently apply your handbrake
- ○ c  Firmly use your footbrake
- ○ d  Coast into the bend
- ○ e  Avoid sudden steering movements

## Q199

Before starting a journey in freezing weather you should clear ice and snow from your vehicle's

*Mark four answers*

- ○ a  aerial
- ○ b  windows
- ○ c  bumper
- ○ d  lights
- ○ e  mirrors
- ○ f  number plates

## Q200

You are braking on a wet road. Your vehicle begins to skid. Your vehicle does not have anti-lock brakes. What is the FIRST thing you should do?

*Mark one answer*

- ○ a  Quickly pull up the handbrake
- ○ b  Release the footbrake fully
- ○ c  Push harder on the brake pedal
- ○ d  Gently use the accelerator

## Q201

How can you tell when you are driving over black ice?

*Mark one answer*

- ○ a  It is easier to brake
- ○ b  The noise from your tyres sounds louder
- ○ c  You see black ice on the road
- ○ d  Your steering feels light

## Q202

Coasting the vehicle

*Mark one answer*

- ○ a  improves the driver's control
- ○ b  makes steering easier
- ○ c  reduces the driver's control
- ○ d  uses more fuel

### Q203

You are turning left on a slippery road. The back of your vehicle slides to the right. You should

*Mark one answer*

- a   brake firmly and not turn the steering wheel
- b   steer carefully to the left
- c   steer carefully to the right
- d   brake firmly and steer to the left

### Q204

You are trying to move off on snow. You should use

*Mark one answer*

- a   the lowest gear you can
- b   the highest gear you can
- c   a high engine speed
- d   the handbrake and footbrake together

### Q205

When driving in falling snow you should

*Mark one answer*

- a   brake firmly and quickly
- b   be ready to steer sharply
- c   use sidelights only
- d   brake gently in plenty of time

### Q206

The MAIN benefit of having four-wheel drive is to improve

*Mark one answer*

- a   road holding
- b   fuel consumption
- c   stopping distances
- d   passenger comfort

### Q207

When driving in fog in daylight you should use

*Mark one answer*

- a   sidelights
- b   full beam headlights
- c   hazard lights
- d   dipped headlights

### Q208

You are at a junction with limited visibility. You should

*Mark one answer*

- a   inch forward, looking to the right
- b   inch forward, looking to the left
- c   inch forward, looking both ways
- d   be ready to move off quickly

### Q209

In very hot weather the road surface can get soft. Which TWO of the following will be affected most?

*Mark two answers*

- a   The suspension
- b   The steering
- c   The braking
- d   The windscreen

### Q210

You are on a long, downhill slope. What should you do to help control the speed of your vehicle?

*Mark one answer*

- a   Select neutral
- b   Select a lower gear
- c   Grip the handbrake firmly
- d   Apply the parking brake gently

## Q211

Where are you most likely to be affected by a sidewind?

*Mark one answer*

- a   On a narrow country lane
- b   On an open stretch of road
- c   On a busy stretch of road
- d   On a long, straight road

## Q212

Your indicators may be difficult to see in bright sunlight. What should you do?

*Mark one answer*

- a   Put your indicator on earlier
- b   Give an arm signal as well as using your indicator
- c   Touch the brake several times to show the stop lamps
- d   Turn as quickly as you can

## Q213

You are about to go down a steep hill. To control the speed of your vehicle you should

*Mark one answer*

- a   select a high gear and use the brakes carefully
- b   select a high gear and use the brakes firmly
- c   select a low gear and use the brakes carefully
- d   select a low gear and avoid using the brakes

## Q214

You are driving in falling snow. Your wipers are not clearing the windscreen. You should

*Mark one answer*

- a   set the windscreen demister to cool
- b   be prepared to clear the windscreen by hand
- c   use the windscreen washers
- d   partly open the front windows

## Q215

When driving on snow it is best to keep in as high a gear as possible. Why is this?

*Mark one answer*

- a   To help you slow down quickly when you brake
- b   So that the wheelspin does not cause your engine to run too fast
- c   To leave a lower gear available in case of wheelspin
- d   To help to prevent wheelspin

## Q216

You wish to park facing DOWNHILL. Which TWO of the following should you do?

*Mark two answers*

- a   Turn the steering wheel towards the kerb
- b   Park close to the bumper of another car
- c   Park with two wheels on the kerb
- d   Put the handbrake on firmly
- e   Turn the steering wheel away from the kerb

## Q217

In windy conditions you need to take extra care when

*Mark one answer*
- ○ a   using the brakes
- ○ b   making a hill start
- ○ c   turning into a narrow road
- ○ d   passing pedal cyclists

## Q218

You are driving in a built-up area. You approach a speed hump. You should

*Mark one answer*
- ○ a   move across to the left-hand side of the road
- ○ b   wait for any pedestrians to cross
- ○ c   slow your vehicle right down
- ○ d   stop and check both pavements

## Q219

How can you use the engine of your vehicle as a brake?

*Mark one answer*
- ○ a   By changing to a lower gear
- ○ b   By selecting reverse gear
- ○ c   By changing to a higher gear
- ○ d   By selecting neutral gear

## Q220

When approaching a right-hand bend you should keep well to the left. Why is this?

*Mark one answer*
- ○ a   To improve your view of the road
- ○ b   To overcome the effect of the road's slope
- ○ c   To let faster traffic from behind overtake
- ○ d   To be positioned safely if the vehicle skids

## Q221

You are coming up to a right-hand bend. You should

*Mark one answer*
- ○ a   keep well to the left as it makes the bend faster
- ○ b   keep well to the left for a better view around the bend
- ○ c   keep well to the right to avoid anything in the gutter
- ○ d   keep well to the right to make the bend less sharp

## Q222

You should not overtake when

*Mark three answers*

- ○ a   intending to turn left shortly afterwards
- ○ b   in a one-way street
- ○ c   approaching a junction
- ○ d   driving up a long hill
- ○ e   the view ahead is blocked

### Answers and Explanations

Q162  b

Q163  c  You should brake rapidly and firmly.

Q164  b

Q165  d

Q166  b  A vehicle fitted with anti-lock brakes is very difficult, but not impossible, to skid. Take care if the road surface is loose or wet.

Q167  b, c

Q168  c

Q169  c

Q170  b, c

Q171  c

Q172  b

Q173  b

Q174  b

Q175  a  Note this is the braking distance. The overall stopping distance is further because you have to add 'thinking' distance.

Q176  b

Q177  d

Q178  b

Q179  c

Q180  a, c, e

Q181  a  This is the 'two-second' rule.

Q182  a

Q183  c

Q184  c

Q185  b

Q186  b

Q187  a  Remember that you and your passenger are flung forwards when you brake hard, which is one reason why you need to wear a seat belt.

Q188  d  This problem is sometimes called aquaplaning. Your tyres build up a thin film of water between them and the road and lose all grip. The steering suddenly feels light and probably uncontrollable. The solution is to ease off the accelerator until you feel the tyres grip the road again.

Q189  d  Your brakes may be wet. The first thing you should do is check them and then dry them.

Q190  d  Drive slowly forwards with your left foot gently on the footbrake. This helps dry out the brakes.

Q191  d

Q192  d

Q193  d

Q194  a  Wheelspin is caused by too much acceleration. The less grip the tyres have on the road, the more wheel spin is likely, and on icy roads the tyres have very little grip. A slow speed is essential and a high gear keeps the wheels turning more gently for the speed.

Q195  a

Q196 **b** Skidding is usually caused by harsh braking, harsh acceleration or harsh steering – all actions of the driver. You are, however, more likely to cause a skid in a poorly maintained car, in bad weather or on a poor road surface.

Q197 **c**

Q198 **a, e** Braking on an icy bend is extremely dangerous. It could cause your vehicle to spin.

Q199 **b, d, e, f**

Q200 **b** Note that the question asks for the first thing you should do, which is always to remove the cause of the skid – in this case braking. You would next need to re-apply the brakes more gently. 'c' is wrong because braking harder would increase the skid.

Q201 **d** Black ice is normally invisible when you are driving. The tyres will lose grip with the road which will make the steering feel light.

Q202 **c** Coasting means driving along with the clutch pedal down. This disconnects the engine and gears from the drive wheels of the car, so you have less control.

Q203 **c**

Q204 **b** A higher gear helps avoid wheelspin.

Q205 **d**

Q206 **a**

Q207 **d** Sidelights are not enough so 'a' is wrong. Full beam headlights tend to reflect back the fog, so 'b' is also incorrect.

Q208 **c** You cannot go until you can see that it is safe, so you need to inch forward until you can see clearly in both directions.

Q209 **b, c**

Q210 **b** You should ideally have selected the lower gear before starting down the slope. 'a' would be likely to make your car go faster as you would no longer be in any gear at all.

Q211 **b**

Q212 **b**

Q213 **c** A low gear will help control your speed, but on a steep hill you will also need your brakes.

Q214 **b** Bear in mind that you would have to stop first.

Q215 **d**

Q216 **a, d** If the handbrake should fail, the car will roll into the kerb and not down the road.

Q217 **d** In windy conditions cyclists are all too easily blown about and may wobble or steer off course.

Q218 **c**

Q219 **a**

Q220 **a** You can see further round the bend earlier if you keep to the left.

Q221 **b**

Q222 **a, c, e**

**Driving Theory Test Questions**

# Hazard Perception

## Q223

You see this sign on the rear of a slow-moving lorry that you want to pass. It is travelling in the middle lane of a three lane motorway. You should

*Mark one answer*

- a cautiously approach the lorry then pass on either side
- b follow the lorry until you can leave the motorway
- c wait on the hard shoulder until the lorry has stopped
- d approach with care and keep to the left of the lorry

## Q224

Where would you expect to see these markers?

*Mark two answers*

- a On a motorway sign
- b At the entrance to a narrow bridge
- c On a large goods vehicle
- d On a builder's skip placed on the road

## Q225

What does this signal from a police officer mean to oncoming traffic?

*Mark one answer*

- a Go ahead
- b Stop
- c Turn left
- d Turn right

## Q226

What is the main hazard shown in this picture?

*Mark one answer*

- a Vehicles turning right
- b Vehicles doing U-turns
- c The cyclist crossing the road
- d Parked cars around the corner

## Q227

Which road user has caused a hazard?

*Mark one answer*

- ○ a The parked car (arrowed A)
- ○ b The pedestrian waiting to cross (arrowed B)
- ○ c The moving car (arrowed C)
- ○ d The car turning (arrowed D)

## Q228

What should the driver of the car approaching the crossing do?

*Mark one answer*

- ○ a Continue at the same speed
- ○ b Sound the horn
- ○ c Drive through quickly
- ○ d Slow down and get ready to stop

## Q229

What should the driver of the red car do?

*Mark one answer*

- ○ a Wave the pedestrians who are waiting to cross
- ○ b Wait for the pedestrian in the road to cross
- ○ c Quickly drive behind the pedestrian in the road
- ○ d Tell the pedestrian in the road she should not have crossed

## Q230

What THREE things should the driver of the grey car (arrowed) be especially aware of?

*Mark three answers*

- ○ a Pedestrians stepping out between cars
- ○ b Other cars behind the grey car
- ○ c Doors opening on parked cars
- ○ d The bumpy road surface
- ○ e Cars leaving parking spaces
- ○ f Empty parking spaces

## Q231

What should the driver of the red car (arrowed) do?

*Mark one answer*

- a Sound the horn to tell other drivers where he is
- b Squeeze through the gap
- c Wave the driver of the white car to go on
- d Wait until the car blocking the way has moved

## Q232

What should the driver of the grey car (arrowed) do?

*Mark one answer*

- a Cross if the way is clear
- b Reverse out of the box junction
- c Wait in the same place until the lights are green
- d Wait until the lights are red then cross

## Q233

What should the driver of a car coming up to this level crossing do?

*Mark one answer*

- a Drive through quickly
- b Drive through carefully
- c Stop before the barrier
- d Switch on hazard warning lights

## Q234

What are TWO main hazards a driver should be aware of when driving along this street?

*Mark two answers*

- a Glare from the sun
- b Car doors opening suddenly
- c Lack of road markings
- d The headlights on parked cars being switched on
- e Large goods vehicles
- f Children running out from between vehicles

What is the main hazard a driver should be aware of when following this cyclist?

*Mark one answer*

- ○ a  The cyclist may move into the left and dismount
- ○ b  The cyclist may swerve out into the road
- ○ c  The contents of the cyclist's carrier may fall onto the road
- ○ d  The cyclist may wish to turn right at the end of the road

The driver of which car has caused a hazard?

*Mark one answer*

- ○ a  Car A
- ○ b  Car B
- ○ c  Car C
- ○ d  Car D

You think the driver of the vehicle in front has forgotten to cancel the right indicator. You should

*Mark one answer*

- ○ a  flash your lights to alert the driver
- ○ b  sound your horn before overtaking
- ○ c  overtake on the left if there is room
- ○ d  stay behind and not overtake

What is the main hazard the driver of the red car (arrowed) should be most aware of?

*Mark one answer*

- ○ a  Glare from the sun may affect the driver's vision
- ○ b  The black car may stop suddenly
- ○ c  The bus may move out into the road
- ○ d  Oncoming vehicles will assume the driver is turning right

In heavy motorway traffic you are being followed closely by the vehicle behind. How can you lower the risk of an accident?

*Mark one answer*

- ○ a   Increase your distance from the vehicle in front
- ○ b   Tap your foot on the brake pedal
- ○ c   Switch on your hazard lights
- ○ d   Move onto the hard shoulder and stop

As a provisional licence holder, you must not drive a motor car

*Mark two answers*

- ○ a   at more than 50 mph
- ○ b   on your own
- ○ c   on the motorway
- ○ d   under the age of 18 years of age at night
- ○ e   with passengers in the rear seats

You are driving along this dual carriageway. Why may you need to slow down?

*Mark one answer*

- ○ a   There is a broken white line in the centre
- ○ b   There are solid white lines either side
- ○ c   There are roadworks ahead of you
- ○ d   There are no footpaths

What does the solid white line at the side of the road indicate?

*Mark one answer*

- ○ a   Traffic lights ahead
- ○ b   Edge of the carriageway
- ○ c   Footpath on the left
- ○ d   Cycle path

Q243

You see this sign ahead. You should expect the road to

*Mark one answer*
- a go steeply uphill
- b go steeply downhill
- c bend sharply to the left
- d bend sharply to the right

Q244

You are approaching this cyclist. You should

*Mark one answer*
- a overtake before the cyclist gets to the junction
- b flash your headlights at the cyclist
- c slow down and allow the cyclist to turn
- d overtake the cyclist on the left-hand side

Q245

You have just been overtaken by this motorcyclist who is cutting in sharply. You should

*Mark one answer*
- a sound the horn
- b brake firmly
- c keep a safe gap
- d remember to flash your lights

Q246

Why must you take extra care when turning right at this junction?

*Mark one answer*
- a Road surface is poor
- b Footpaths are narrow
- c Road markings are faint
- d There is reduced visibility

## Q247

What is the main hazard in this picture?

*Mark one answer*

- a  The pedestrian
- b  The parked cars
- c  The junction on the left
- d  The driveway on the left

## Q248

You are driving towards this parked lorry. What is the first hazard you should be aware of?

*Mark one answer*

- a  The lorry moving off
- b  The narrowing road
- c  The pedestrian crossing
- d  The vehicles ahead

## Q249

This yellow sign on a vehicle indicates this is

*Mark one answer*

- a  a vehicle broken down
- b  a school bus
- c  an ice cream van
- d  a private ambulance

## Q250

You are driving towards this level crossing. What would be the first warning of an approaching train?

*Mark one answer*

- a  Both half barriers down
- b  A steady amber light
- c  One half barrier down
- d  Twin flashing red lights

You are driving along this motorway. It is raining. When following this lorry you should

*Mark two answers*

○ a  allow at least a two-second gap
○ b  move left and drive on the hard shoulder
○ c  allow at least a four-second gap
○ d  be aware of spray reducing your vision
○ e  move right and stay in the right hand lane

You are behind this cyclist. When the traffic lights change, what should you do?

*Mark one answer*

○ a  Try to move off before the cyclist
○ b  Allow the cyclist time and room
○ c  Turn right but give the cyclist room
○ d  Tap your horn and drive through first

You are driving towards this left hand bend. What dangers should you be aware of?

*Mark one answer*

○ a  A vehicle overtaking you
○ b  No white lines in the centre of the road
○ c  No sign to warn you of the bend
○ d  Pedestrians walking towards you

When approaching this bridge you should give way to

*Mark one answer*

○ a  bicycles
○ b  buses
○ c  motorcycles
○ d  cars

## Q255

What type of vehicle could you expect to meet in the middle of the road?

*Mark one answer*
- ○ a    Lorry
- ○ b    Bicycle
- ○ c    Car
- ○ d    Motorcycle

## Q256

As the driver of this vehicle, why should you slow down?

*Mark two answers*
- ○ a    Because of the bend
- ○ b    Because it's hard to see to the right
- ○ c    Because of approaching trains
- ○ d    Because of animals crossing
- ○ e    Because of the level crossing

## Q257

While driving, you see this sign ahead. You should

*Mark one answer*
- ○ a    stop at the sign
- ○ b    slow, but continue around the bend
- ○ c    slow to a crawl and continue
- ○ d    stop and look for open farm gates

## Q258

Why should the junction on the left be kept clear?

*Mark one answer*
- ○ a    To allow vehicles to enter and emerge
- ○ b    To allow the bus to reverse
- ○ c    To allow vehicles to make a 'U' turn
- ○ d    To allow vehicles to park

Q259

What is the first hazard shown in this picture?

*Mark one answer*
- a Standing traffic
- b Oncoming traffic
- c Junction on the left
- d Pedestrians

Q260

You are driving in the left lane but want to turn right at the traffic lights. You should

*Mark one answer*
- a check your mirrors, signal and move to the right
- b weave into the middle and then to the right lane
- c drive up to the lights then turn right
- d stay in your lane and find another way back

Q261

When the traffic lights change to green the white car should

*Mark one answer*
- a wait for the cyclist to pull away
- b move off quickly and turn in front of the cyclist
- c move close up to the cyclist to beat the lights
- d sound the horn to warn the cyclist

Q262

You intend to turn left at the traffic lights. Just before turning you should

*Mark one answer*
- a check your right mirror
- b move close up to the white car
- c straddle the lanes
- d check for bicycles on your left

## Q263

You should reduce your speed when driving along this road because

*Mark one answer*
- a   there is a staggered junction ahead
- b   there is a low bridge ahead
- c   there is a change in the road surface
- d   the road ahead narrows

## Q264

An approaching motorcyclist is easier to see when

*Mark three answers*
- a   the rider is wearing bright clothing
- b   the rider has a white helmet
- c   the headlight is on
- d   the motorcyle is moving slowly
- e   the motorcyle is moving quickly
- f   the rider has a passenger

## Q265

You are driving at 60 mph. As you approach this hazard you should

*Mark one answer*
- a   maintain your speed
- b   reduce your speed
- c   take the next right turn
- d   take the next left turn

## Q266

The traffic ahead of you in the left lane is slowing. You should

*Mark two answers*
- a   be wary of cars on your right cutting in
- b   accelerate past the vehicles in the left lane
- c   pull up on the left hand verge
- d   move across and continue in the right hand lane
- e   slow down keeping a safe separation distance

**Q267**

You are driving on a road with several lanes. You see these signs above the lanes. What do they mean?

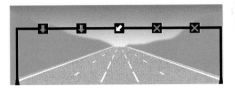

*Mark one answer*

- a  The two right lanes are open
- b  The two left lanes are open
- c  Traffic in the left lanes should stop
- d  Traffic in the right lanes should stop

**Q268**

At this blind junction you must stop

*Mark one answer*

- a  behind the line, then edge forward to see clearly
- b  beyond the line at a point where you can see clearly
- c  only if there is traffic on the main road
- d  only if you are turning to the right

**Q269**

When must you stop at this junction?

*Mark one answer*

- a  During rush hour only
- b  Only when the area is busy
- c  When turning right only
- d  At all times

**Q270**

What might you expect to happen in this situation?

*Mark one answer*

- a  Traffic will move into the right-hand lane
- b  Traffic speed will increase
- c  Traffic will move into the left-hand lane
- d  Traffic will not need to change position

## Answers and Explanations

| | |
|---|---|
| Q223 | d |
| Q224 | c, d |
| Q225 | b |
| Q226 | c |
| Q227 | a |
| Q228 | d |
| Q229 | b |
| Q230 | a, c, e |
| Q231 | d |
| Q232 | a |
| Q233 | c |
| Q234 | b, f |
| Q235 | b |
| Q236 | a |
| Q237 | d |
| Q238 | c |
| Q239 | a |
| Q240 | b, c |
| Q241 | c |
| Q242 | b |
| Q243 | c |
| Q244 | c |
| Q245 | c |
| Q246 | d |
| Q247 | a |
| Q248 | c |
| Q249 | b |
| Q250 | b |
| Q251 | c, d |
| Q252 | b |
| Q253 | d |
| Q254 | b |
| Q255 | a |
| Q256 | a, e |
| Q257 | b |
| Q258 | a |
| Q259 | c |
| Q260 | d |

| | |
|---|---|
| Q261 | a |
| Q262 | d |
| Q263 | a |
| Q264 | a, b, c |
| Q265 | b |
| Q266 | a, e |
| Q267 | b |
| Q268 | a |
| Q269 | d |
| Q270 | c |

**Driving Theory Test Questions**

# Impairment

## Q271

To drive you MUST be able to read a number plate from what distance?

*Mark one answer*

- a 10 metres (32 feet)
- b 15 metres (50 feet)
- c 20.5 metres (67 feet)
- d 25.5 (84 feet)

## Q272

You find that you need glasses to read vehicle number plates. When MUST you wear them?

*Mark one answer*

- a Only in bad weather conditions
- b At all times when driving
- c Only when you think it necessary
- d Only in bad light or at night time

## Q273

A driver can only read a number plate at the required distance with glasses on. The glasses should be worn

*Mark one answer*

- a all the time when driving
- b only when driving long distances
- c only when reversing
- d only in poor visibility

## Q274

How does alcohol affect your driving?

*Mark one answer*

- a It speeds up your reactions
- b It increases your awareness
- c It improves your co-ordination
- d It reduces your concentration

## Q275

You are about to drive home. You cannot find the glasses you need to wear when driving. You should

*Mark one answer*

- a drive home slowly, keeping to quiet roads
- b borrow a friend's glasses and drive home
- c drive home at night, so that the lights will help you
- d find a way of getting home without driving

## Q276

Which THREE result from drinking alcohol and driving?

*Mark three answers*

- a Less control
- b A false sense of confidence
- c Faster reactions
- d Poor judgement of speed
- e Greater awareness of danger

## Q277

You go to a social event and need to drive a short time after. What precaution should you take?

*Mark one answer*

- a Avoid drinking alcohol on an empty stomach
- b Drink plenty of coffee after drinking alcohol
- c Avoid drinking alcohol completely
- d Drink plenty of milk before drinking alcohol

## Q278

Which THREE of these are likely effects of drinking alcohol on driving?

*Mark three answers*

- a  Reduced co-ordination
- b  Increased confidence
- c  Poor judgement
- d  Increased concentration
- e  Faster reactions
- f  Colour blindness

## Q279

You MUST wear glasses or contact lenses when driving on public roads if

*Mark one answer*

- a  you are the holder of an orange badge
- b  you cannot read a vehicle number plate from a distance of 36 metres (120 feet) without them
- c  there is an eyesight problem in your family
- d  you cannot read a vehicle number plate from a distance of 20.5 metres (67 feet) without them

## Q280

As a driver you find that your eyesight has become very poor. Your optician says he cannot help you. The law says that you should tell

*Mark one answer*

- a  the licensing authority
- b  your own doctor
- c  the local police station
- d  another optician

## Q281

After passing your driving test, you suffer from ill health. This affects your driving. You MUST

*Mark one answer*

- a  inform your local police station
- b  get on as best you can
- c  not inform anyone as you hold a full licence
- d  inform the licensing authority

## Q282

Drinking any amount of alcohol is likely to

*Mark three answers*

- a  slow down your reactions to hazards
- b  increase the speed of your reactions
- c  worsen your judgement of speed
- d  improve your awareness of danger
- e  give a false sense of confidence

## Q283

You are invited to a pub lunch. You know that you will have to drive in the evening. What is your best course of action?

*Mark one answer*

- a  Avoid mixing your alcoholic drinks
- b  Not drink any alcohol at all
- c  Have some milk before drinking alcohol
- d  Eat a hot meal with your alcoholic drinks

## Q284

What else can seriously affect your concentration when driving, other than alcoholic drinks?

*Mark three answers*
- a Drugs
- b Tiredness
- c Tinted windows
- d Contact lenses
- e Loud music

## Q285

After drinking alcohol heavily you should not drive the following day. Why is this?

*Mark two answers*
- a You may still be over the legal limit
- b Your concentration will not be badly affected
- c You will be well under the legal limit
- d Your concentration may still be badly affected

## Q286

You have been convicted of driving whilst unfit through drink or drugs. You will find this is likely to cause the cost of one of the following to rise considerably. Which one?

*Mark one answer*
- a Road fund licence
- b Insurance premiums
- c Vehicle test certificate
- d Driving licence

## Q287

What advice should you give to a driver who has had a few alcoholic drinks at a party?

*Mark one answer*
- a Have a strong cup of coffee and then drive home
- b Drive home carefully and slowly
- c Go home by public transport
- d Wait a short while and then drive home

## Q288

It is eight hours since you last had an alcoholic drink. Which of the following applies?

*Mark two answers*
- a You will certainly be under the legal limit
- b You will have no alcohol in your system
- c You may still be unfit to drive
- d You may still be over the legal limit

## Q289

Your doctor has given you a course of medicine. Why should you ask if it is OK to drive?

*Mark one answer*
- a Drugs make you a better driver by quickening your reactions
- b You will have to let your insurance company know about the medicine
- c Some types of medicine can cause your reactions to slow down
- d The medicine you take may affect your hearing

## Q290

You have been taking medicine for a few days which made you feel drowsy. Today you feel better but still need to take the medicine. You should only drive

*Mark one answer*

○ a  if your journey is necessary
○ b  at night on quiet roads
○ c  if someone goes with you
○ d  after checking with your doctor

## Q291

You are about to return home from holiday when you become ill. A doctor prescribes drugs which are likely to affect your driving. You should

*Mark one answer*

○ a  drive only if someone is with you
○ b  avoid driving on motorways
○ c  not drive yourself
○ d  never drive at more than 30 mph

## Q292

During periods of illness your ability to drive may be impaired. You MUST

*Mark two answers*

○ a  see your doctor each time before you drive
○ b  only take smaller doses of any medicines
○ c  be medically fit to drive
○ d  not drive after taking certain medicines
○ e  take all your medicines with you when you drive

## Q293

You are not sure if your cough medicine will affect your driving. What TWO things could you do?

*Mark two answers*

○ a  Ask your doctor
○ b  Check the medicine label
○ c  Drive if you feel alright
○ d  Ask a friend or relative for advice

## Q294

You take some cough medicine given to you by a friend. What should you do before driving?

*Mark one answer*

○ a  Ask your friend if taking the medicine affected their driving
○ b  Drink some strong coffee one hour before driving
○ c  Check the label to see if the medicine will affect your driving
○ d  Drive a short distance to see if the medicine is affecting your driving

## Q295

You have taken medication that may make you feel drowsy. Your friends tell you it is safe to drive. What should you do?

*Mark one answer*

○ a  Take their advice and drive
○ b  Ignore your friends' advice and do not drive
○ c  Only drive if they come with you
○ d  Drive for short distances only

**Q296**

You feel drowsy when driving. You should

*Mark two answers*
- a stop and rest as soon as possible
- b turn the heater up to keep you warm and comfortable
- c make sure you have a good supply of fresh air
- d continue with your journey but drive more slowly
- e close the car windows to help you concentrate

**Q297**

You are driving along a motorway and become tired. You should

*Mark two answers*
- a stop at the next service area and rest
- b leave the motorway at the next exit and rest
- c increase your speed and turn up the radio volume
- d close all your windows and set heating to warm
- e pull up on the hard shoulder and change drivers

**Q298**

You are taking drugs that are likely to affect your driving. What should you do?

*Mark one answer*
- a Seek medical advice before driving
- b Limit your driving to essential journeys
- c Only drive if accompanied by a full licence-holder
- d Drive only for short distances

**Q299**

You are about to drive home. You feel very tired and have a severe headache. You should

*Mark one answer*
- a wait until you are fit and well before driving
- b drive home, but take a tablet for headaches
- c drive home if you can stay awake for the journey
- d wait for a short time, then drive home slowly

**Q300**

If you are feeling tired it is best to stop as soon as you can. Until then you should

*Mark one answer*
- a increase your speed to find a stopping place quickly
- b ensure a supply of fresh air
- c gently tap the steering wheel
- d keep changing speed to improve concentration

**Q301**

You are driving on a motorway. You feel tired. You should

*Mark one answer*
- a carry on but drive slowly
- b leave the motorway at the next exit
- c complete your journey as quickly as possible
- d stop on the hard shoulder

## Q302

You are planning a long journey. It should take about six hours. Do you need to plan rest stops?

*Mark one answer*

- a Yes, you should plan to stop after about four hours driving
- b Yes, regular stops help concentration
- c No, you will be less tired if you get there as soon as possible
- d No, only fuel stops will be needed

## Q303

Driving long distances can be tiring. You can prevent this by

*Mark three answers*

- a stopping every so often for a walk
- b opening a window for some fresh air
- c ensuring plenty of refreshment breaks
- d completing the journey without stopping
- e eating a large meal before driving

## Q304

Which TWO things would help to keep you alert during a long journey?

*Mark two answers*

- a Finishing your journey as fast as you can
- b Keeping off the motorways and using country roads
- c Making sure that you get plenty of fresh air
- d Making regular stops for refreshments

## Q305

Which THREE are likely to make you lose concentration while driving?

*Mark three answers*

- a Looking at road maps
- b Listening to loud music
- c Using your windscreen washers
- d Looking in your wing mirror
- e Using a mobile phone

## Q306

An elderly person's driving ability could be affected because they may be unable to

*Mark one answer*

- a obtain car insurance
- b understand road signs
- c react very quickly
- d give signals correctly

## Q307

Your reactions will be much slower when driving

*Mark one answer*

- a if tired
- b in fog
- c too quickly
- d in rain

## Q308

To help concentration on long journeys you should stop frequently and

*Mark one answer*

- a have a rest
- b fill up with fuel
- c eat a meal
- d take a shower

## Q309

If your motorway journey seems boring and you feel drowsy whilst driving you should

*Mark one answer*

- ○ a open a window and drive to the next service area
- ○ b stop on the hard shoulder for a sleep
- ○ c speed up to arrive at your destination sooner
- ○ d slow down and let other drivers overtake

## Answers and Explanations

Q271 **c** Glasses or contact lenses may be worn.

Q272 **b** If you need glasses to drive you must wear them whenever you are driving, so 'b' is correct.

Q273 **a**

Q274 **d** You may well feel, after drinking, that 'a', 'b' and 'c' are true. However, this is never correct and makes you dangerous.

Q275 **d** It is illegal to drive if you cannot satisfy the requirements of the eyesight test.

Q276 **a, b, d**

Q277 **c**

Q278 **a, b, c**

Q279 **d**

Q280 **a** You must not drive if your eyesight becomes so poor that you can no longer meet the minimum legal requirements, wearing glasses or contact lenses if necessary.

Q281 **d** In the event of a short-term illness, like flu, that affected your ability to drive, you would simply not drive until you are recovered.

Q282 **a, c, e**

Q283 **b**

Q284 **a, b, e**

Q285 **a, d** Alcohol takes many hours to pass through your system.

Q286 **b**

Q287 **c** The only sensible answer is don't drink and drive.

Q288 **c, d**

Q289 **c**

Q290 **d**

Q291 **c**

Q292 **c, d**

Q293 **a, b**

Q294 **c**

Q295 **b**

Q296 **a, c**

Q297 **a, b**

Q298 **a** A significant number of drugs, even those you can buy in the chemist, can affect your ability to drive. Sometimes a warning is given on the packet, but if in any doubt seek medical advice.

Q299 **a**

Q300 **b**

Q301 **b** If you feel tired you greatly increase your chances of having an accident. You must stop, but as you are on a motorway you cannot do this unless you leave

at the next exit or find a service
station before it.

Q302  b

Q303  a, b, c

Q304  c, d

Q305  a, b, e 'c' and 'd' are normal parts
of the driving task.

Q306  c

Q307  a

Q308  a

Q309  a

**Driving Theory Test Questions**

# Other Road Users

## Q310

You are driving on a country road. What should you expect to see coming towards you on YOUR side of the road?

*Mark one answer*

- a  Motorcycles
- b  Bicycles
- c  Pedestrians
- d  Horse riders

## Q311

Which sign means that there may be people walking along the road?

*Mark one answer*

- a
- b
- c
- d

## Q312

What does this sign mean?

*Mark one answer*

- a  Pedestrian crossing
- b  Pedestrians in the road ahead
- c  No pedestrians
- d  Route for pedestrians

## Q313

You are turning left into a side road. Pedestrians are crossing the road near the junction. You must

*Mark one answer*

- a  wave them on
- b  sound your horn
- c  switch on your hazard lights
- d  wait for them to cross

## Q314

You are turning left at a junction. Pedestrians have started to cross the road. You should

*Mark one answer*

- a  go on, giving them plenty of room
- b  stop and wave at them to cross
- c  blow your horn and proceed
- d  give way to them

## Q315

You are turning left from a main road into a side road. People are already crossing the road into which you are turning. You should

*Mark one answer*

- a  continue, as it is your right of way
- b  signal to them to continue crossing
- c  wait and allow them to cross
- d  sound your horn to warn them of your presence

## Q316

You are at a road junction, turning into a minor road. There are pedestrians crossing the minor road. You should

*Mark one answer*

- a  stop and wave the pedestrians across
- b  sound your horn to let the pedestrians know that you are there
- c  give way to the pedestrians who are already crossing
- d  carry on; the pedestrians should give way to you

## Q317

You are turning left into a side road. What hazards should you be especially aware of?

*Mark one answer*

- a  One way street
- b  Pedestrians
- c  Traffic congestion
- d  Parked vehicles

## Q318

You want to reverse into a side road. You are not sure that the area behind your car is clear. What should you do?

*Mark one answer*

- a  Look through the rear window only
- b  Get out and check
- c  Check the mirrors only
- d  Carry on, assuming it is clear

## Q319

You are about to reverse into a side road. A pedestrian wishes to cross behind you. You should

*Mark one answer*

- a  wave to the pedestrian to stop
- b  give way to the pedestrian
- c  wave to the pedestrian to cross
- d  reverse before the pedestrian starts to cross

## Q320

Who is especially in danger of not being seen as you reverse your car?

*Mark one answer*
- a Motorcyclists
- b Car drivers
- c Cyclists
- d Children

## Q321

You are reversing around a corner when you notice a pedestrian walking behind you. What should you do?

*Mark one answer*
- a Slow down and wave the pedestrian across
- b Continue reversing and steer round the pedestrian
- c Stop and give way
- d Continue reversing and sound your horn

## Q322

You want to turn right from a junction but your view is restricted by parked vehicles. What should you do?

*Mark one answer*
- a Move out quickly, but be prepared to stop
- b Sound your horn and pull out if there is no reply
- c Stop, then move slowly forward until you have a clear view
- d Stop, get out and look along the main road to check

## Q323

You intend to turn right into a side road. Just before turning you should check for motorcyclists who might be

*Mark one answer*
- a overtaking on your left
- b following you closely
- c emerging from the side road
- d overtaking on your right

## Q324

You are at the front of a queue of traffic waiting to turn right into a side road. Why is it important to check your right mirror just before turning?

*Mark one answer*
- a To look for pedestrians about to cross
- b To check for overtaking vehicles
- c To make sure the side road is clear
- d To check for emerging traffic

## Q325

In which THREE places would parking your vehicle cause danger or obstruction to other road users?

*Mark three answers*
- a In front of a property entrance
- b At or near a bus stop
- c On your driveway
- d In a marked parking space
- e On the approach to a level crossing

### Q326

As you approach a pelican crossing the lights change to green. Elderly people are halfway across. You should

*Mark one answer*

- ○ a   wave them to cross as quickly as they can
- ○ b   rev your engine to make them hurry
- ○ c   flash your lights in case they have not heard you
- ○ d   wait because they will take longer to cross

### Q327

In which three places would parking cause an obstruction to others?

*Mark three answers*

- ○ a   Near the brow of a hill
- ○ b   In a lay-by
- ○ c   Where the kerb is raised
- ○ d   Where the kerb has been lowered for wheelchairs
- ○ e   At or near a bus stop

### Q328

What must a driver do at a pelican crossing when the amber light is flashing?

*Mark one answer*

- ○ a   Signal the pedestrian to cross
- ○ b   Always wait for the green light before proceeding
- ○ c   Give way to any pedestrians on the crossing
- ○ d   Wait for the red-and-amber light before proceeding

### Q329

You have stopped at a pelican crossing. A disabled person is crossing slowly in front of you. The lights have now changed to green. You should

*Mark two answers*

- ○ a   allow the person to cross
- ○ b   drive in front of the person
- ○ c   drive behind the person
- ○ d   sound your horn
- ○ e   be patient
- ○ f   edge forward slowly

### Q330

A toucan crossing is different from other crossings because

*Mark one answer*

- ○ a   moped riders can use it
- ○ b   it is controlled by a traffic warden
- ○ c   it is controlled by two flashing lights
- ○ d   cyclists can use it

### Q331

At toucan crossings

*Mark two answers*

- ○ a   there is no flashing amber light
- ○ b   cyclists are not permitted
- ○ c   there is a continuously flashing amber beacon
- ○ d   pedestrians and cyclists may cross
- ○ e   you only stop if someone is waiting to cross

## Q332

Look at this picture. What is the danger you should be most aware of?

*Mark one answer*

○ a   The ice cream van may move off
○ b   The driver of the ice cream van may get out
○ c   The car on the left may move off
○ d   The child may run out into the road

## Q333

Which age group is most likely to be involved in a road accident?

*Mark one answer*

○ a   36 to 45-year-olds
○ b   55-year-olds and over
○ c   46 to 55-year-olds
○ d   17 to 25-year-olds

## Q334

You should NEVER attempt to overtake a cyclist

*Mark one answer*

○ a   just before you turn left
○ b   just before you turn right
○ c   on a one-way street
○ d   on a dual carriageway

## Q335

You are driving past parked cars. You notice a wheel of a bicycle sticking out between them. What should you do?

*Mark one answer*

○ a   Accelerate past quickly and sound your horn
○ b   Slow down and wave the cyclist across
○ c   Brake sharply and flash your headlights
○ d   Slow down and be prepared to stop for a cyclist

## Q336

You are driving past a line of parked cars. You notice a ball bouncing out into the road ahead. What should you do?

*Mark one answer*

○ a   Continue driving at the same speed and sound your horn
○ b   Continue driving at the same speed and flash your headlights
○ c   Slow down and be prepared to stop for children
○ d   Stop and wave the children across to fetch their ball

**Q337**

What does this sign tell you?

*Mark one answer*

- a No cycling
- b Cycle route ahead
- c Route for cycles only
- d End of cycle route

**Q338**

How will a school crossing patrol signal you to stop?

*Mark one answer*

- a By pointing to children on the opposite pavement
- b By displaying a red light
- c By displaying a stop sign
- d By giving you an arm signal

**Q339**

You see a pedestrian carrying a white stick. This shows that the person is

*Mark one answer*

- a disabled
- b deaf
- c elderly
- d blind

**Q340**

You are approaching a school crossing patrol. When this sign is held up you must

*Mark one answer*

- a stop and allow any children to cross
- b stop and beckon the children to cross
- c stop only if the children are on a pedestrian crossing
- d stop only when the children are actually crossing the road

**Q341**

Where would you see this sign?

*Mark one answer*

- a In the window of a car taking children to school
- b At the side of the road
- c At playground areas
- d On the rear of a school bus or coach

## Q342

Where would you see this sign?

*Mark one answer*

- a   On the approach to a school crossing
- b   At a playground entrance
- c   On a school bus
- d   At a 'pedestrians only' area

## Q343

You are parking your vehicle in the street. The car parked in front of you is displaying an orange badge. You should

*Mark one answer*

- a   park close to it to save road space
- b   allow room for a wheelchair
- c   wait until the orange-badge holder returns
- d   park with two wheels on the pavement

## Q344

You are following a car driven by an elderly driver. You should

*Mark one answer*

- a   expect the driver to drive badly
- b   flash your lights and overtake
- c   be aware that the driver's reactions may not be as fast as yours
- d   stay close behind and drive carefully

## Q345

Which sign tells you that pedestrians may be walking in the road as there is no pavement?

*Mark one answer*

 a

 b

 c

 d

## Q346

Which sign means there may be elderly pedestrians likely to cross the road ?

*Mark one answer*

 a

 b

 a

 b

 c

 d

**Q347**

What does this sign mean?

*Mark one answer*

- a No route for pedestrians and cyclists
- b A route for pedestrians only
- c A route for cyclists only
- d A route for pedestrians and cyclists

**Q348**

You see a pedestrian with a white stick and red band. This means that the person is

*Mark one answer*

- a physically disabled
- b deaf only
- c blind only
- d deaf and blind

**Q349**

You are driving towards a zebra crossing. Waiting to cross is a person in a wheelchair. You should

*Mark one answer*

- a continue on your way
- b wave to the person to cross
- c wave to the person to wait
- d be prepared to stop

**Q350**

What action would you take when elderly people are crossing the road?

*Mark one answer*

- a Wave them across so they know that you have seen them
- b Be patient and allow them to cross in their own time
- c Rev the engine to let them know that you are waiting
- d Tap the horn in case they are hard of hearing

**Q351**

You see two elderly pedestrians about to cross the road ahead. You should

*Mark one answer*

- a expect them to wait for you to pass
- b speed up to get past them quickly
- c stop and wave them across the road
- d be careful, they may misjudge your speed

## Q352

You are following a motorcyclist on an uneven road. You should

*Mark one answer*
- a  allow less room to ensure that you can be seen in their mirrors
- b  overtake immediately
- c  allow extra room in case they swerve to avoid pot-holes
- d  allow the same room as normal because motorcyclists are not affected by road surfaces

## Q353

What does this sign mean?

*Mark one answer*
- a  Contra-flow pedal cycle lane
- b  With-flow pedal cycle lane
- c  Pedal cycles and buses only
- d  No pedal cycles or buses

## Q354

Which TWO should you allow extra room when overtaking?

*Mark two answers*
- a  Motorcycles
- b  Tractors
- c  Bicycles
- d  Road-sweeping vehicles

## Q355

You are driving behind a cyclist. You wish to turn left just ahead. You should

*Mark one answer*
- a  overtake the cyclist before the junction
- b  pull alongside the cyclist and stay level until after the junction
- c  hold back until the cyclist has passed the junction
- d  go around the cyclist on the junction

## Q356

You are driving behind two cyclists. They approach a roundabout in the left-hand lane. In which direction should you expect the cyclists to go?

*Mark one answer*
- a  Left
- b  Right
- c  Any direction
- d  Straight ahead

**Q357**

You are coming up to a roundabout. A cyclist is signalling to turn right. What should you do?

*Mark one answer*

- a Overtake on the right
- b Give a horn warning
- c Signal the cyclist to move across
- d Give the cyclist plenty of room

**Q358**

You are approaching this roundabout and see the cyclist signal right. Why is the cyclist keeping to the left?

*Mark one answer*

- a It is a quicker route for the cyclist
- b The cyclist is going to turn left instead
- c The cyclist thinks *The Highway Code* does not apply to bicycles
- d The cyclist is slower and more vulnerable

**Q359**

When you are overtaking a cyclist you should leave as much room as you would give to a car. What is the main reason for this?

*Mark one answer*

- a The cyclist might change lanes
- b The cyclist might get off the bike
- c The cyclist might swerve
- d The cyclist might have to make a right turn

**Q360**

Why should you allow extra room when overtaking a motorcyclist on a windy day?

*Mark one answer*

- a The rider may turn off suddenly to get out of the wind
- b The rider may be blown across in front of you
- c The rider may stop suddenly
- d The rider may be travelling faster than normal

**Q361**

Which type of vehicle is most affected by strong winds?

*Mark one answer*

- a Tractor
- b Motorcycle
- c Car
- d Tanker

### Q362

Why should you look particularly for motorcyclists and cyclists at junctions?

*Mark one answer*

- a They may want to turn into the side road
- b They may slow down to let you turn
- c They are harder to see
- d They might not see you turn

### Q363

You are waiting to come out of a side road. Why should you watch carefully for motorcycles?

*Mark one answer*

- a Motorcycles are usually faster than cars
- b Police patrols often use motorcycles
- c Motorcycles are small and hard to see
- d Motorcycles have right of way

### Q364

Where should you take particular care to look out for motorcyclists and cyclists?

*Mark one answer*

- a On dual carriageways
- b At junctions
- c At zebra crossings
- d On one-way streets

### Q365

In daylight, an approaching motorcyclist is using a dipped headlight. Why?

*Mark one answer*

- a So that the rider can be seen more easily
- b To stop the battery overcharging
- c To improve the rider's vision
- d The rider is inviting you to proceed

### Q366

Where in particular should you look out for motorcyclists?

*Mark one answer*

- a In a filling station
- b At a road junction
- c Near a service area
- d When entering a car park

### Q367

Motorcycle riders are vulnerable because they

*Mark one answer*

- a are easy for other road users to see
- b are difficult for other road users to see
- c are likely to have breakdowns
- d cannot give arm signals

## Q368

Motorcyclists should wear bright clothing mainly because

*Mark one answer*

- a   they must do so by law
- b   it helps keep them cool in summer
- c   the colours are popular
- d   drivers often do not see them

## Q369

At road junctions which of the following are most vulnerable?

*Mark three answers*

- a   Cyclists
- b   Motorcyclists
- c   Pedestrians
- d   Car drivers
- e   Lorry drivers

## Q370

Motorcyclists ride in daylight with their headlights switched on because

*Mark one answer*

- a   it is a legal requirement
- b   there is a speed trap ahead
- c   they need to be seen
- d   there are speed humps ahead

## Q371

There is a slow-moving motorcyclist ahead of you. You are unsure what the rider is going to do. You should

*Mark one answer*

- a   pass on the left
- b   pass on the right
- c   stay behind
- d   move closer

## Q372

Motorcyclists will often look round over their right shoulder just before turning right. This is because

*Mark one answer*

- a   they need to listen for following traffic
- b   motorcycles do not have mirrors
- c   looking around helps them balance as they turn
- d   they need to check for traffic in their blind area

## Q373

You are driving behind a moped. You want to turn left just ahead. You should

*Mark one answer*

- a   overtake the moped before the junction
- b   pull alongside the moped and stay level until just before the junction
- c   sound your horn as a warning and pull in front of the moped
- d   stay behind until the moped has passed the junction

## Q374

When emerging from a side road into a queue of traffic, which vehicles can be especially difficult to see?

*Mark one answer*

- a   Motorcycles
- b   Tractors
- c   Milk floats
- d   Cars

## Q375

You want to turn right from a main road into a side road. Just before turning you should

*Mark one answer*
- a    cancel your right-turn signal
- b    select first gear
- c    check for traffic overtaking on your right
- d    stop and set the handbrake

## Q376

How should you overtake horse riders?

*Mark one answer*
- a    Drive up close and overtake as soon as possible
- b    Speed is not important but allow plenty of room
- c    Use your horn just once to warn them
- d    Drive slowly and leave plenty of room

## Q377

Which of the following are hazards motorcyclists present in queues of traffic?

*Mark three answers*
- a    Cutting in just in front of you
- b    Riding in single file
- c    Passing very close to your car
- d    Riding with their headlamp on dipped beam
- e    Filtering between the lanes

## Q378

You are driving on a main road. You intend to turn right into a side road. Just before turning you should

*Mark one answer*
- a    adjust your interior mirror
- b    flash your headlamps
- c    steer over to the left
- d    check for traffic overtaking on your offside

## Q379

How would you react to other drivers who appear to be inexperienced?

*Mark one answer*
- a    Sound your horn to warn them of your presence
- b    Be patient and prepared for them to react more slowly
- c    Flash your headlights to indicate that it is safe for them to proceed
- d    Overtake them as soon as possible

## Q380

Motorcyclists are particularly vulnerable

*Mark one answer*

- a   when moving off
- b   on dual carriageways
- c   when approaching junctions
- d   on motorways

## Q381

When driving, ahead of you there is a vehicle with a flashing amber beacon. This means it is

*Mark one answer*

- a   slow moving
- b   broken down
- c   a doctor's car
- d   a school crossing patrol

## Q382

You are driving in town. There is a bus at the bus stop on the other side of the road. Why should you be careful?

*Mark one answer*

- a   The bus may have broken down
- b   Pedestrians may come from behind the bus
- c   The bus may move off suddenly
- d   The bus may remain stationary

## Q383

Your vehicle hits a pedestrian at 40 mph. The pedestrian will

*Mark one answer*

- a   certainly be killed
- b   certainly survive
- c   probably be killed
- d   probably survive

## Q384

You are driving on a narrow country road. Where would you find it most difficult to see horses and riders ahead of you?

*Mark one answer*

- a   On left-hand bends
- b   When travelling downhill
- c   When travelling uphill
- d   On right-hand bends

## Q385

A horse rider is in the left-hand lane approaching a roundabout. The driver behind should expect the rider to

*Mark one answer*

- a   go in any direction
- b   turn right
- c   turn left
- d   go ahead

## Q386

You are driving in slow-moving queues of traffic. Just before changing lane you should

*Mark one answer*

- a   sound the horn
- b   look for motorcyclists filtering through the traffic
- c   give a 'slowing down' arm signal
- d   change down to first gear

## Q387

You are approaching a roundabout. There are horses just ahead of you. You should

*Mark two answers*
- a  be prepared to stop
- b  treat them like any other vehicle
- c  give them plenty of room
- d  accelerate past as quickly as possible
- e  sound your horn as a warning

## Q388

You see some horse riders as you approach a roundabout. They are signalling right but keeping well to the left. You should

*Mark one answer*
- a  proceed as normal
- b  keep close to them
- c  cut in front of them
- d  stay well back

## Q389

Which THREE should you do when passing sheep on a road?

*Mark three answers*
- a  Allow plenty of room
- b  Drive very slowly
- c  Pass quickly but quietly
- d  Be ready to stop
- e  Briefly sound your horn

## Q390

What is the most common factor in causing road accidents?

*Mark one answer*
- a  Weather conditions
- b  Driver error
- c  Road conditions
- d  Mechanical failure

## Q391

A friend wants to teach you to drive a car. They must

*Mark one answer*
- a  be over 21 and have held a full licence for at least two years
- b  be over 18 and hold an advanced driver's certificate
- c  be over 18 and have fully comprehensive insurance
- d  be over 21 and have held a full licence for at least three years

## Q392

At night you see a pedestrian wearing reflective clothing and carrying a bright red light. What does this mean?

*Mark one answer*
- a  You are approaching roadworks
- b  You are approaching an organised walk
- c  You are approaching a slow-moving vehicle
- d  You are approaching an accident blackspot

**Q393**

You have a collision whilst your car is moving. What is the first thing you must do?

*Mark one answer*

- a   Stop only if there are injured people
- b   Call the emergency services
- c   Stop at the scene of the accident
- d   Call your insurance company

**Q394**

As a new driver, how can you decrease your risk of accidents on the motorway?

*Mark one answer*

- a   By keeping up with the car in front
- b   By never driving over 45 mph
- c   By driving only in the nearside lane
- d   By taking further training

**Q395**

You are following a learner driver who stalls at a junction. You should

*Mark one answer*

- a   be patient as you expect them to make mistakes
- b   drive up close behind and flash your headlamps
- c   start to rev your engine if they take too long to restart
- d   immediately steer around them and drive on

**Q396**

You are dazzled at night by a vehicle behind you. You should

*Mark one answer*

- a   set your mirror to anti dazzle
- b   set your mirror to dazzle the other driver
- c   brake sharply to a stop
- d   switch your rear lights on and off

**Q397**

You notice horse riders in front. What should you do FIRST?

*Mark one answer*

- a   Pull out to the middle of the road
- b   Be prepared to slow down
- c   Accelerate around them
- d   Signal right

## Answers and Explanations

**Q310** c Pedestrians are the most likely to expect as country roads often have no pavements and pedestrians are advised to walk on the right so that they can see oncoming traffic on their side of the road. However, you should always expect the unexpected when driving.

**Q311** d Red triangles give warnings, in this case of people walking along the road. 'c' is a warning of a pedestrian crossing.

**Q312** c

**Q313** d When you turn into a side road pedestrians who are already crossing have priority so you must give way.

**Q314** d

**Q315** c

**Q316** c

**Q317** b

**Q318** b

**Q319** b

**Q320** d Children are small and you may not be able to see them through your rear windscreen.

**Q321** c

**Q322** c You cannot turn right until you can see it is safe to do so. You should stop and then edge slowly forwards until you can see clearly to the left and right.

**Q323** d

**Q324** b

**Q325** a, b, e

**Q326** d

**Q327** a, d, e

**Q328** c

**Q329** a, e

**Q330** d

**Q331** a, d

**Q332** d

**Q333** d

**Q334** a The word 'NEVER' makes 'a' correct.

**Q335** d

**Q336** c

**Q337** b

**Q338** c

**Q339** d

**Q340** a

**Q341** d

**Q342** c

**Q343** b

**Q344** c

**Q345** a

**Q346** a

**Q347** d

**Q348** d

**Q349** d

**Q350** b

**Q351** d The ability to judge speed tends to deteriorate as you get older.

**Q352** c

**Q353** b

**Q354** a, c Motorcycles and bicycles can easily swerve and you need to allow them extra room.

**Q355** c As the question states you are turning left JUST ahead, you have no time to overtake the cyclist safely which is why 'c' is correct.

**Q356** c

**Q357** d

**Q358** d

**Q359** c 'c' is the answer required, but you should also be aware that cyclists can be unpredictable.

Q360  b

Q361  b

Q362  c

Q363  c

Q364  b

Q365  a

Q366  b

Q367  b

Q368  d

Q369  a, b, c

Q370  c

Q371  c

Q372  d

Q373  d

Q374  a

Q375  c  Use your right door mirror and look particularly for motorcyclists.

Q376  d

Q377  a, c, e  Check your door mirrors, especially before moving forwards or changing lanes.

Q378  d

Q379  b

Q380  c

Q381  a

Q382  b

Q383  c  When pedestrians are about 'kill your speed'.

Q384  a  'a' is correct. However, remember that narrow country roads often have banks, hedges, trees or other obstructions to your view as well as bends so look out on right hand bends as well.

Q385  a

Q386  b

Q387  a, c

Q388  d

Q389  a, b, d

Q390  b  Statistics show that about 95% of accidents involve an element of human error.

Q391  d

Q392  b

Q393  c

Q394  d

Q395  a

Q396  a

Q397  b  Horses and their riders can be unpredictable so 'b' is the safest first action.

**Driving Theory Test Questions**

# Other Vehicle Characteristics

## Q398

The road is wet. Why might a motorcyclist steer round drain covers on a bend?

*Mark one answer*

- ○ a   To avoid puncturing the tyres on the edge of the drain covers
- ✗ b   To prevent the motorcycle sliding on the metal drain covers
- ○ c   To help judge the bend using the drain covers as marker points
- ○ d   To avoid splashing pedestrians on the pavement

## Q399

It is very windy. You are behind a motorcyclist who is overtaking a high-sided vehicle. What should you do?

*Mark one answer*

- ○ a   Overtake the motorcyclist immediately
- ✗ b   Keep well back
- ○ c   Stay level with the motorcyclist
- ○ d   Keep close to the motorcyclist

## Q400

It is very windy. You are about to overtake a motorcyclist. You should

*Mark one answer*

- ○ a   overtake slowly
- ✗ b   allow extra room
- ○ c   sound your horn
- ○ d   keep close as you pass

## Q401

You are about to overtake a slow-moving motorcyclist. Which one of these signs would make you take special care?

*Mark one answer*

- ✗ a
- ○ b
- ○ c
- ○ d

## Q402

You are waiting to emerge left from a minor road. A large vehicle is approaching from the right. You have time to turn, but you should wait. Why?

*Mark one answer*

- ✗ a   The large vehicle can easily hide an overtaking vehicle
- ○ b   The large vehicle can turn suddenly
- ○ c   The large vehicle is difficult to steer in a straight line
- ○ d   The large vehicle can easily hide vehicles from the left

## Q403

You are following a large articulated vehicle. It is going to turn left into a narrow road. What action should you take?

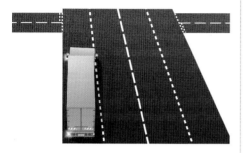

*Mark one answer*

- ○ a   Move out and overtake on the offside
- ○ b   Pass on the left as the vehicle moves out
- ⊘ c   Be prepared to stop behind
- ○ d   Overtake quickly before the lorry moves out

## Q404

You are following a long vehicle. It approaches a crossroads and signals left, but moves out to the right. You should

*Mark one answer*

- ○ a   get closer in order to pass it quickly
- ⊘ b   stay well back and give it room
- ○ c   assume the signal is wrong and it is really turning right
- ○ d   overtake as it starts to slow down

## Q405

You are following a long vehicle approaching a crossroads. The driver signals right but moves close to the left-hand kerb. What should you do?

*Mark one answer*

- ○ a   Warn the driver of the wrong signal
- ⊘ b   Wait behind the long vehicle
- ○ c   Report the driver to the police
- ○ d   Overtake on the right-hand side

## Q406

You are approaching a mini-roundabout. The long vehicle in front is signalling left but positioned over to the right. You should

*Mark one answer*

- ○ a   sound your horn
- ○ b   overtake on the left
- ○ c   follow the same course as the lorry
- ⊘ d   keep well back

## Q407

You are following a large vehicle. Side and end markers are being displayed. This means the load

*Mark one answer*
- ○ a   is higher than normal
- ○ b   may be flammable
- ⊘ c   is in two parts
- ○ d   overhangs at the rear   ✗

## Q408

You are towing a caravan. Which is the safest type of rear view mirror to use?

*Mark one answer*
- ○ a   Interior wide-angle-view mirror
- ⊘ b   Extended-arm side mirrors
- ○ c   Ordinary door mirrors
- ○ d   Ordinary interior mirror

## Q409

You keep well back while waiting to overtake a large vehicle. Another car fills the gap. You should

*Mark one answer*
- ○ a   sound your horn
- ⊘ b   drop back further
- ○ c   flash your headlights
- ○ d   start to overtake

## Q410

Before overtaking a large vehicle you should keep well back. Why is this?

*Mark one answer*
- ○ a   To give acceleration space to overtake quickly on blind bends
- ⊘ b   To get the best view of the road ahead
- ○ c   To leave a gap in case the vehicle stops and rolls back
- ○ d   To offer other drivers a safe gap if they want to overtake you

## Q411

You wish to overtake a long, slow moving vehicle on a busy road. You should

*Mark one answer*
- ○ a   follow it closely and keep moving out to see the road ahead
- ○ b   flash your headlights for the oncoming traffic to give way
- ○ c   stay behind until the driver waves you past
- ⊘ d   keep well back until you can see that it is clear

## Q412

You are driving downhill. There is a car parked on the other side of the road. Large, slow lorries are coming towards you. You should

✗

*Mark one answer*
- ⊘ a   keep going because you have the right of way
- ○ b   slow down and give way
- ○ c   speed up and get past quickly
- ○ d   pull over on the right behind the parked car

## Q413

When about to overtake a long vehicle you should

*Mark one answer*

- a sound the horn to warn the driver that you are there
- b stay well back from the lorry to obtain a better view
- c drive close to the lorry in order to pass more quickly
- d flash your lights and wait for the driver to signal when it is safe

## Q414

Why is passing a lorry more risky than passing a car?

*Mark one answer*

- a Lorries are longer than cars
- b Lorries may suddenly pull up
- c The brakes of lorries are not as good
- d Lorries climb hills more slowly

## Q415

As a driver, why should you be more careful where trams operate?

*Mark two answers*

- a Because they do not have a horn
- b Because they do not stop for cars
- c Because they are silent
- d Because they cannot steer to avoid you
- e Because they do not have lights

## Q416

You are driving along a road and you see this signal. It means

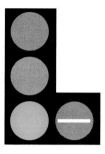

*Mark one answer*

- a cars must stop
- b trams must stop
- c both trams and cars must stop
- d both trams and cars can continue

## Q417

You are travelling behind a bus that pulls up at a bus stop. What should you do?

*Mark two answers*

- a Accelerate past the bus sounding your horn
- b Watch carefully for pedestrians
- c Be ready to give way to the bus
- d Pull in closely behind the bus

## Q418

You are driving on a wet motorway with surface spray. You should use

*Mark one answer*

- a your hazard flashers
- b dipped headlights
- c your rear fog lights
- d your sidelights

## Q419

You are driving in town. Ahead of you a bus is at a bus stop. Which two of the following should you do?

*Mark two answers*

- ✏ a  Be prepared to give way if the bus suddenly moves off
- ○ b  Continue at the same speed but sound your horn as a warning
- ✏ c  Watch carefully for the sudden appearance of pedestrians
- ○ d  Pass the bus as quickly as you possibly can

## Q420

When you approach a bus signalling to move off from a bus stop you should

*Mark one answer*

- ○ a  get past before it moves
- ✏ b  allow it to pull away, if it is safe to do so
- ○ c  flash your headlights as you approach
- ○ d  signal left and wave the bus on

## Q421

Which of these vehicles is LEAST likely to be affected by crosswinds?

*Mark one answer*

- ○ a  Cyclists
- ○ b  Motorcyclists
- ○ c  High-sided vehicles
- ✏ d  Cars

## Q422

What does 'tailgating' mean?

*Mark one answer*

- ○ a  When a vehicle delivering goods has its tailgate down
- ○ b  When a vehicle is travelling with its back doors open
- ✏ c  When a driver is following another vehicle too closely
- ○ d  When stationary vehicles are too close in a queue

## Q423

You are driving in heavy traffic on a wet road. Spray makes it difficult to be seen. You should use your

*Mark two answers*

- ○ a  full beam headlights
- ✏ b  rear fog lights if visibility is less than 100 metres (328 feet)
- ○ c  rear fog lights if visibility is more than 100 metres (328 feet)
- ✏ d  dipped headlights
- ○ e  side lights only

## Q424

Some two way roads are divided into three lanes. Why are these particularly dangerous?

*Mark one answer*

- a   Traffic in both directions can use the middle lane to overtake
- b   Traffic can travel faster in poor weather conditions
- c   Traffic can overtake on the left
- d   Traffic uses the middle lane for emergencies only

## Q425

You are following a large lorry on a wet road. Spray makes it difficult to see. You should

*Mark one answer*

- a   drop back until you can see better
- b   put your headlights on full beam
- c   keep close to the lorry, away from the spray
- d   speed up and overtake quickly

Q398   b   Water on metal is a dangerous combination, especially for a two-wheeled vehicle.

Q399   b   Let the motorcyclist complete the overtake before even thinking about following.

Q400   b   Motorcycles may have problems with strong crosswinds.

Q401   a   The motorcyclist may wobble as you pass by in a windy situation.

Q402   a

Q403   c   The large articulated vehicle may need to position to the right in order to turn left into the narrow road.

Q404   b

Q405   b   Long vehicles require more space to turn and often need to position for this.

Q406   d

Q407   d

Q408   b

Q409   b

Q410   b   You cannot see ahead if you are too close to a large vehicle in front of you.

Q411   d

Q412   b

Q413   b

Q414   a   Overtaking takes time, so the longer the vehicle you overtake the greater the danger, as you will take longer to pass it.

Q415   c, d

Q416   b

Q417   b, c

Q418   b   Spray reduces visibility. You should use dipped headlights when visibility is reduced.

Q419   a, c
Q420   b   This helps traffic flow without giving confusing signals.
Q421   d   Of the four mentioned, cars are by far the most stable and least affected by crosswinds.
Q422   c
Q423   b, d
Q424   a
Q425   a

**Driving Theory Test Questions**

# Own Vehicle Handling

## Q426

You should avoid 'coasting' your vehicle because it could

*Mark one answer*
- a damage the suspension
- b increase tyre wear
- c flatten the battery
- d reduce steering control

## Q427

Why is coasting wrong?

*Mark one answer*
- a It will cause the car to skid
- b It will make the engine stall
- c The engine will run faster
- d There is no engine braking

## Q428

Hills can affect the performance of your vehicle. Which TWO apply when driving up steep hills?

*Mark two answers*
- a Higher gears will pull better
- b You will slow down sooner
- c Overtaking will be easier
- d The engine will work harder
- e The steering will feel heavier

## Q429

You are approaching a bend at speed. You should begin to brake

*Mark one answer*
- a on the bend
- b after the bend
- c after changing gear
- d before the bend

## Q430

What are TWO main reasons why coasting downhill is wrong?

*Mark two answers*
- a Fuel consumption will be higher
- b The vehicle will pick up speed
- c It puts more wear and tear on the tyres
- d You have less braking and steering control
- e It damages the engine

## Q431

You are following a vehicle at a safe distance on a wet road. Another driver overtakes you and pulls into the gap you have left. What should you do?

*Mark one answer*
- a Flash your headlights as a warning
- b Try to overtake safely as soon as you can
- c Drop back to regain a safe distance
- d Stay close to the other vehicle until it moves on

## Q432

You are driving in the left-hand lane of a dual carriageway. Another vehicle overtakes and pulls in front of you leaving you without enough separation distance. You should

*Mark one answer*
- a move to the right-hand lane
- b continue as you are
- c drop back
- d sound your horn

### Q433

In which THREE of these situations may you overtake another vehicle on the left?

*Mark three answers*

- a When you are in a one-way street
- b When approaching a motorway slip road where you will be turning off
- c When the vehicle in front is signalling to turn right
- d When a slower vehicle is travelling in the right-hand lane of a dual carriageway
- e In slow-moving traffic queues when traffic in the right-hand lane is moving more slowly

### Q434

You are driving on the motorway in windy conditions. When passing high-sided vehicles you should

*Mark one answer*

- a increase your speed
- b be wary of a sudden gust
- c drive alongside very closely
- d expect normal conditions

### Q435

Which THREE of the following will affect your stopping distance?

*Mark three answers*

- a How fast you are going
- b The tyres on your vehicle
- c The time of day
- d The weather
- e The street lighting

### Q436

You are travelling in very heavy rain. Your overall stopping distance is likely to be

*Mark one answer*

- a doubled
- b halved
- c up to ten times greater
- d no different

### Q437

Motorcyclists are more at risk from other road users because they

*Mark one answer*

- a are less experienced than other drivers
- b are more likely to break down than other motorists
- c are always faster than other drivers
- d are more difficult to see than other drivers

### Q438

You have to make a journey in fog. What are the TWO most important things you should do before you set out?

*Mark two answers*

- a Top up the radiator with antifreeze
- b Make sure that you have a warning triangle in the vehicle
- c Check that your lights are working
- d Check the battery
- e Make sure that the windows are clean

### Q439

When snow is falling heavily you should

*Mark one answer*

- a drive as long as your headlights are used
- b not drive unless you have a mobile phone
- c drive only when your journey is short
- d not drive unless it is essential

### Q440

Why should you test your brakes after this hazard?

*Mark one answer*

- a Because you will be driving on a slippery road
- b Because your brakes will be soaking wet
- c Because you will have driven down a long hill
- d Because you will have just crossed a long bridge

### Q441

You are driving on an icy road. What distance should you drive from the car in front?

*Mark one answer*

- a Eight times the normal distance
- b Six times the normal distance
- c Ten times the normal distance
- d Four times the normal distance

### Q442

Front fog lights may be used ONLY

*Mark one answer*

- a if they are not as bright as the headlights
- b when visibility is seriously reduced
- c between dusk and dawn
- d during 'lighting up' times only

### Q443

You are driving in very wet weather. Your vehicle begins to slide. This effect is called

*Mark one answer*

- a hosing
- b weaving
- c aquaplaning
- d fading

### Q444

Using front fog lights in clear daylight will

*Mark one answer*

- a flatten the battery
- b dazzle other drivers
- c improve your visibility
- d increase your awareness

## Q445

You have to make a journey in foggy conditions. You should

*Mark one answer*

- a  follow closely other vehicles' tail lights
- b  never use demisters and windscreen wipers
- c  leave plenty of time for your journey
- d  keep two seconds behind other vehicles

## Q446

Front fog lights may be used ONLY if

*Mark one answer*

- a  visibility is seriously reduced
- b  they are fitted above the bumper
- c  they are not as bright as the headlights
- d  an audible warning device is used

## Q447

Front fog lights may be used ONLY if

*Mark one answer*

- a  your headlights are not working
- b  they are operated with rear fog lights
- c  they were fitted by the vehicle manufacturer
- d  visibility is seriously reduced

## Q448

Front fog lights may be used ONLY if

*Mark one answer*

- a  they prevent headlight glare on a wet road
- b  you wish to overtake in bad weather
- c  visibility is seriously reduced
- d  fitted by the manufacturer

## Q449

You may drive with front fog lights switched on

*Mark one answer*

- a  when visibility is less than 100 metres (328 feet)
- b  at any time to be noticed
- c  instead of headlights on high speed roads
- d  when dazzled by the lights of oncoming vehicles

## Q450

Front fog lights should be used ONLY when

*Mark one answer*

- a travelling in very light rain
- b visibility is seriously reduced
- c daylight is fading
- d driving after midnight

## Q451

Front fog lights should be used

*Mark one answer*

- a when visibility is reduced to 100 metres (328 feet)
- b as a warning to oncoming traffic
- c when driving during the hours of darkness
- d in any conditions and at any time

## Q452

You may use front fog lights with headlights ONLY when visibility is reduced to less than

*Mark one answer*

- a 100 metres (328 feet)
- b 200 metres (656 feet)
- c 300 metres (984 feet)
- d 400 metres (1312 feet)

## Q453

Using rear fog lights in clear daylight will

*Mark one answer*

- a be useful when towing a trailer
- b give extra protection
- c dazzle other drivers
- d make following drivers keep back

## Q454

You are following other vehicles in fog with your lights on. How else can you reduce the chances of being involved in an accident?

*Mark one answer*

- a Keep close to the vehicle in front
- b Use your main beam instead of dipped headlights
- c Keep together with the faster vehicles
- d Reduce your speed and increase the gap

## Q455

Why should you always reduce your speed when driving in fog?

*Mark one answer*

- a Because the brakes do not work as well
- b Because you could be dazzled by other people's fog lights
- c Because the engine's colder
- d Because it is more difficult to see events ahead

## Q456

You are driving in fog. Why should you keep well back from the vehicle in front?

*Mark one answer*

- a In case it changes direction suddenly
- b In case its fog lights dazzle you
- c In case it stops suddenly
- d In case its brake lights dazzle you

**Q457**

You should switch your rear fog lights on when visibility drops below

*Mark one answer*

- a  your overall stopping distance
- b  ten car lengths
- c  200 metres (656 feet)
- d  100 metres (328 feet)

**Q458**

You should only use rear fog lights when you cannot see further than about

*Mark one answer*

- a  100 metres (328 feet)
- b  200 metres (656 feet)
- c  250 metres (820 feet)
- d  150 metres (492 feet)

**Q459**

You should use rear fog lights when

*Mark one answer*

- a  vehicles are following too closely
- b  visibility is reduced to 100 metres (328 feet)
- c  very bright sunshine is dazzling motorists
- d  driving in busy, fast-moving traffic

**Q460**

Whilst driving, the fog clears and you can see more clearly. You must remember to

*Mark one answer*

- a  switch off the fog lights
- b  reduce your speed
- c  switch off the demister
- d  close any open windows

**Q461**

You are driving on a clear, dry night with your rear fog lights switched on. This may

*Mark two answers*

- a  reduce glare from the road surface
- b  make other drivers think you are braking
- c  give a better view of the road ahead
- d  dazzle following drivers
- e  help your indicators to be seen more clearly

**Q462**

Why is it dangerous to leave rear fog lights on when they are not needed?

*Mark two answers*

- a  Brake lights are less clear
- b  Following drivers can be dazzled
- c  Electrical systems could be overloaded
- d  Direction indicators may not work properly
- e  The battery could fail

**Q463**

You are driving in thick fog using fog lights. When visibility improves you MUST

*Mark one answer*

- a  maintain your speed
- b  keep them on
- c  increase your speed
- d  switch them off

## Q464

You have just driven out of fog. Visibility is now good. You MUST

*Mark one answer*
- a   switch off all your fog lights
- b   keep your rear fog lights on
- c   keep your front fog lights on
- d   leave fog lights on in case fog returns

## Q465

You forget to switch off your rear fog lights when the fog has cleared. This may

*Mark three answers*
- a   dazzle other road users
- b   reduce battery life
- c   cause brake lights to be less clear
- d   be breaking the law
- e   seriously affect engine power

## Q466

You are driving on a well-lit motorway at night. You must

*Mark one answer*
- a   use only your sidelights
- b   always use your headlights
- c   always use rear fog lights
- d   use headlights only in bad weather

## Q467

You see a vehicle coming towards you on a single-track road. You should

*Mark one answer*
- a   reverse back to the main road
- b   do an emergency stop
- c   stop at a passing place
- d   put on your hazard warning lights

## Q468

You have been driving in thick fog which has now cleared. You must switch OFF your rear fog lights because

*Mark one answer*
- a   they use a lot of power from the battery
- b   they make your brake lights less clear
- c   they will cause dazzle in your rear view mirrors
- d   they may not be properly adjusted

## Q469

Front and rear fog lights MUST be

*Mark one answer*
- a   connected to an audible warning signal
- b   used outside built up areas only
- c   switched off in night-time fog
- d   switched off if visibility is not seriously reduced

## Q470

While you are driving in fog, it becomes necessary to use front fog lights. You should

*Mark one answer*
- a   only turn them on in heavy traffic conditions
- b   remember not to use them on motorways
- c   only use them with dipped headlights
- d   remember to switch them off as visibility improves

## Q471

You are driving with your front fog lights switched on. Earlier fog has now cleared. What should you do?

*Mark one answer*

- ○ a Leave them on if other drivers have their lights on
- ○ b Switch them off as long as visibility remains good
- ○ c Flash them to warn oncoming traffic that it is foggy
- ○ d Drive with them on instead of your headlights

## Q472

You have to park on the road in fog. You should

*Mark one answer*

- ○ a leave sidelights on
- ○ b leave dipped headlights and fog lights on
- ○ c leave dipped headlights on
- ○ d leave main beam headlights on

## Q473

On a foggy day you unavoidably have to park your car on the road. You should

*Mark one answer*

- ○ a leave your headlights on
- ○ b leave your fog lights on
- ○ c leave your sidelights on
- ○ d leave your hazard lights on

## Q474

You are driving on a motorway in fog. The left-hand edge of the motorway can be identified by reflective studs. What colour are they?

*Mark one answer*

- ○ a Green
- ○ b Amber
- ○ c Red
- ○ d White

## Q475

Should lights be used when travelling at night on a well lit motorway?

*Mark one answer*

- ○ a Yes, but only sidelights are needed
- ○ b Yes, dipped headlights are needed
- ○ c No, unless the weather is bad
- ○ d No, lights are not needed

## Q476

You are driving on a motorway at night. You MUST have your headlights switched on unless

*Mark one answer*

- a there are vehicles close in front of you
- b you are travelling below 50 mph
- c the motorway is lit
- d your vehicle is broken down on the hard shoulder

## Q477

You are travelling on a motorway at night with other vehicles just ahead of you. Which lights should you have on?

*Mark one answer*

- a Front fog lights
- b Main beam headlights
- c Sidelights only
- d Dipped headlights

## Q478

Which TWO of the following are correct? When overtaking at night you should

*Mark two answers*

- a wait until a bend so that you can see the oncoming headlights
- b sound your horn twice before moving out
- c be careful because you can see less
- d beware of bends in the road ahead
- e put headlights on full beam

## Q479

You are overtaking a car at night. You must be sure that

*Mark one answer*

- a you flash your headlamps before overtaking
- b your rear fog lights are switched on
- c you have switched your lights to full beam before overtaking
- d you do not dazzle other road users

## Q480

When may you wait in a box junction?

*Mark one answer*

- a When you are stationary in a queue of traffic
- b When approaching a pelican crossing
- c When approaching a zebra crossing
- d When oncoming traffic prevents you turning right

## Q481

A rumble device is designed to

*Mark two answers*
- a  give directions
- b  prevent cattle escaping
- c  alert drivers to low tyre pressure
- d  alert drivers to a hazard
- e  encourage drivers to reduce speed

## Q482

You are travelling at night. You are dazzled by headlights coming towards you. You should

*Mark one answer*
- a  pull down your sun visor
- b  slow down or stop
- c  switch on your main beam headlights
- d  put your hand over your eyes

## Q483

You are dazzled by oncoming headlights when driving at night. What should you do?

*Mark one answer*
- a  Slow down or stop
- b  Brake hard
- c  Drive faster past the oncoming car
- d  Flash your lights

## Q484

To correct a rear wheel skid you should

*Mark one answer*
- a  not steer at all
- b  steer away from it
- c  steer into it
- d  apply your handbrake

## Q485

You are parking on a two way road at night. The speed limit is 40 mph. You should park on the

*Mark one answer*
- a  left with sidelights on
- b  left with no lights on
- c  right with sidelights on
- d  right with dipped headlights on

## Q486

You are on a narrow road at night. A slower-moving vehicle ahead has been signalling right for some time. What should you do?

*Mark one answer*
- a  Overtake on the left
- b  Flash your headlights before overtaking
- c  Signal right and sound your horn
- d  Wait for the signal to be cancelled before overtaking

## Q487

Which TWO are correct? The passing places on a single-track road are

*Mark two answers*
- a  for taking a rest from driving
- b  to pull into if an oncoming vehicle wants to proceed
- c  for stopping and checking your route
- d  to turn the car around in, if you are lost
- e  to pull into if the car behind wants to overtake

## Q488

Which of the following may apply when dealing with this hazard?

*Mark four answers*

- a It could be more difficult in winter
- b Use a low gear and drive slowly
- c Use a high gear to prevent wheelspin
- d Test your brakes afterwards
- e Always switch on fog lamps
- f There may be a depth gauge

## Q489

Which of these plates normally appear with this road sign?

*Mark one answer*

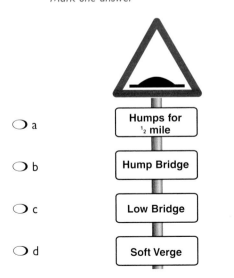

- a **Humps for ½ mile**
- b **Hump Bridge**
- c **Low Bridge**
- d **Soft Verge**

Q426 d

Q427 d You are coasting when you push down the clutch, disconnecting both engine and gear box.

Q428 b, d

Q429 d Avoid braking on a bend. You risk losing the control of your vehicle. Get the speed right before the bend, accelerate gently through the bend and then get the car back up to speed.

Q430 b, d

Q431 c This may feel irritating, particularly if the circumstance is repeated several times. However, it is safest and, in reality, causes no delay.

Q432 c You need to adjust your separation distance continually. Don't get annoyed by this – it keeps you safe and does not add to your journey time.

Q433 a, c, e

Q434 b

Q435 a, b, d

Q436 a

Q437 d

Q438 c, e See and be seen are the two most crucial safety aspects of driving in fog.

Q439 d

Q440 b After driving through water your brakes will be wet, and wet brakes are inefficient.

Q441 c Stopping distances can be up to ten times longer in snow and ice. Give yourself plenty of time to stop.

Q442 b

Q443  c  Surface water builds up a film between the road and the tyres, causing the car to drive on the film of water and not grip the road surface. The steering will feel very light if you are aquaplaning. Release the gas pedal.

Q444  b  You should only use fog lights, front or rear, when visibility is reduced below 100 metres (328 feet).

Q445  c  *The Highway Code* advises you to allow more time for your journey in foggy conditions. However, always ask yourself if the journey really is necessary.

Q446  a

Q447  d

Q448  c

Q449  a

Q450  b

Q451  a

Q452  a

Q453  c  Always remember to switch off your fog lights as soon as visibility improves.

Q454  d

Q455  d  Everybody knows this but an alarming number of people don't put the knowledge into practice. Accidents happen as a result.

Q456  c  If the car in front stops suddenly you may run into it if you have been driving too close.

Q457  d  Remember to switch them off when visibility improves.

Q458  a

Q459  b

Q460  a  Fog lights should only be used where visibility is down to about 100 metres. Otherwise you risk dazzling other drivers.

Q461  b, d

Q462  a, b

Q463  d

Q464  a

Q465  a, c, d

Q466  b

Q467  c  Bear in mind that single-track roads may have passing places at long intervals. You may meet an oncoming vehicle at a point where one of you will need to reverse to the previous nearest passing point.

Q468  b

Q469  d

Q470  d

Q471  b

Q472  a

Q473  c

Q474  c  Red reflective studs separate the left-hand lane and the hard shoulder.

Q475  b

Q476  d  You must use your headlights on motorways at nights even if the motorway is lit.

Q477  d  Full-beam headlights would dazzle the drivers in front by reflecting in their mirrors.

Q478  c, d

Q479  d  You may need to switch to full-beam headlights as you overtake, but not before.

Q480  d  You may wait in a box junction if your exit is clear but oncoming traffic prevents you from turning right.

Q481  d, e  (NB: a rumble device is normally raised strips or markings on the surface of the road.)

Q482  b
Q483  a
Q484  c
Q485  a
Q486  d
Q487  b, e
Q488  a, b, d, f
Q489  a

**Driving Theory Test Questions**

# Roads and Regulations – Motorways

**Q490**

Which of the following CAN travel on a motorway?

*Mark one answer*
○ a Cyclists
○ b Vans
○ c Farm tractors
○ d Learner drivers

**Q491**

As a provisional licence-holder you should not drive a car

*Mark one answer*
○ a over 50 mph
○ b at night
○ c on the motorway
○ d with passengers in rear seats

**Q492**

Which FOUR of these must not use motorways?

*Mark four answers*
○ a Learner car drivers
○ b Motorcycles over 50cc
○ c Double-deck buses
○ d Farm tractors
○ e Horse riders
○ f Cyclists

**Q493**

What is the national speed limit on motorways for cars and motorcycles?

*Mark one answer*
○ a 30 mph
○ b 50 mph
○ c 60 mph
○ d 70 mph

**Q494**

Why is it particularly important to carry out a check on your vehicle before making a long motorway journey?

*Mark one answer*
○ a You will have to do more harsh braking on motorways
○ b Motorway service stations do not deal with breakdowns
○ c The road surface will wear down the tyres faster
○ d Continuous high speeds may increase the risk of your vehicle breaking down

**Q495**

Immediately after joining a motorway you should normally

*Mark one answer*
○ a try to overtake
○ b readjust your mirrors
○ c position your vehicle in the centre lane
○ d keep in the left lane

**Q496**

You are joining a motorway. Why is it important to make full use of the slip road?

*Mark one answer*
○ a Because there is space available to reverse if you need to
○ b To allow you direct access to the overtaking lanes
○ c To build up a speed similar to traffic on the motorway
○ d Because you can continue on the hard shoulder

**Q497**

When joining a motorway you must always

*Mark one answer*

- a use the hard shoulder
- b stop at the end of the acceleration lane
- c come to a stop before joining the motorway
- d give way to traffic already on the motorway

**Q498**

You have just joined a motorway. Which lane would you normally stay in to get used to the higher speeds?

*Mark one answer*

- a Hard shoulder
- b Right hand lane
- c Centre lane
- d Left hand lane

**Q499**

What is the national speed limit for cars and motorcycles in the centre lane of a three-lane motorway?

*Mark one answer*

- a 40 mph
- b 50 mph
- c 60 mph
- d 70 mph

**Q500**

You are towing a trailer on a motorway. What is your maximum speed limit?

*Mark one answer*

- a 40 mph
- b 50 mph
- c 60 mph
- d 70 mph

**Q501**

You are driving a car on a motorway. Unless signs show otherwise you must NOT exceed

*Mark one answer*

- a 50 mph
- b 60 mph
- c 70 mph
- d 80 mph

**Q502**

On a three-lane motorway which lane should you use for normal driving?

*Mark one answer*

- a Left
- b Right
- c Centre
- d Either the right or centre

**Q503**

A basic rule when driving on motorways is

*Mark one answer*

- a use the lane that has least traffic
- b keep to the left lane unless overtaking
- c overtake on the side that is most clear
- d try to keep above 50 mph to prevent congestion

## Q504

You are driving on a three-lane motorway at 70 mph. There is no traffic ahead. Which lane should you use?

*Mark one answer*
- a   Any lane
- b   Middle lane
- c   Right lane
- d   Left lane

## Q505

The left-hand lane on a three-lane motorway is for use by

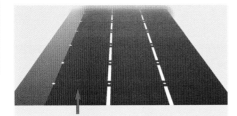

*Mark one answer*
- a   any vehicle
- b   large vehicles only
- c   emergency vehicles only
- d   slow vehicles only

## Q506

You are travelling on a motorway. What colour are the reflective studs on the left of the carriageway?

*Mark one answer*
- a   Green
- b   Red
- c   White
- d   Amber

## Q507

The left-hand lane of a motorway should be used for

*Mark one answer*
- a   breakdowns and emergencies only
- b   overtaking slower traffic in the other lanes
- c   slow vehicles only
- d   normal driving

## Q508

What is the right hand-lane used for on a three-lane motorway?

*Mark one answer*
- a   Emergency vehicles only
- b   Overtaking
- c   Vehicles towing trailers
- d   Coaches only

## Q509

Which of these is NOT allowed to travel in the right-hand lane of a three-lane motorway?

*Mark one answer*
- a   A small delivery van
- b   A motorcycle
- c   A vehicle towing a trailer
- d   A motorcycle and side-car

**Q510**

For what reason may you use the right-hand lane of a motorway?

*Mark one answer*

- a  For keeping out of the way of lorries
- b  For driving at more than 70 mph
- c  For turning right
- d  For overtaking other vehicles

**Q511**

On motorways you should never overtake on the left UNLESS

*Mark one answer*

- a  you can see well ahead that the hard shoulder is clear
- b  the traffic in the right-hand lane is signalling right
- c  you warn drivers behind by signalling left
- d  there is a queue of traffic to your right that is moving more slowly

**Q512**

On a motorway you may ONLY stop on the hard shoulder

*Mark one answer*

- a  in an emergency
- b  If you feel tired and need to rest
- c  if you accidentally go past the exit that you wanted to take
- d  to pick up a hitchhiker

**Q513**

You are travelling on a motorway. You decide you need a rest. You should

*Mark two answers*

- a  stop on the hard shoulder
- b  go to a service area
- c  park on the slip road
- d  park on the central reservation
- e  leave at the next exit

**Q514**

You are driving on a motorway. You have to slow down quickly due to a hazard. You should

*Mark one answer*

- a  switch on your hazard lights
- b  switch on your headlights
- c  sound your horn
- d  flash your headlights

## Q515

You are driving on a motorway. The car ahead shows its hazard lights for a short time. This tells you that

*Mark one answer*
- a   the driver wants you to overtake
- b   the other car is going to change lanes
- c   traffic ahead is slowing or stopping suddenly
- d   there is a police speed check ahead

## Q516

Which vehicles are normally fitted with amber flashing beacons on the roof?

*Mark two answers*
- a   Doctor's car
- b   Bomb disposal team
- c   Blood transfusion team
- d   Breakdown recovery vehicles
- e   Coastguard
- f   Maintenance vehicles

## Q517

You break down on a motorway. You need to call for help. Why may it be better to use an emergency roadside telephone rather than a mobile phone?

*Mark one answer*
- a   It connects you to a local garage
- b   Using a mobile phone will distract other drivers
- c   It allows easy location by the emergency services
- d   Mobile phones do not work on motorways

## Q518

Your vehicle breaks down on the hard shoulder of a motorway. You decide to use your mobile phone to call for help. You should

*Mark one answer*
- a   stand at the rear of the vehicle while making the call
- b   try to repair the vehicle yourself
- c   get out of the vehicle by the right hand door
- d   check your location from the marker posts on the left

## Q519

You get a puncture on the motorway. You manage to get your vehicle onto the hard shoulder. You should

*Mark one answer*
- a   change the wheel yourself immediately
- b   use the emergency telephone and call for assistance
- c   try to wave down another vehicle for help
- d   only change the wheel if you have a passenger to help you

## Q520

The emergency telephones on a motorway are connected to the

*Mark one answer*
- a   ambulance service
- b   police control
- c   fire brigade
- d   breakdown service

**Q521**

How should you use the emergency telephone on a motorway?

*Mark one answer*

- a Stay close to the carriageway
- b Face the oncoming traffic
- c Keep your back to the traffic
- d Keep your head in the kiosk

**Q522**

What should you use the hard shoulder of a motorway for?

*Mark one answer*

- a Stopping in an emergency
- b Leaving the motorway
- c Stopping when you are tired
- d Joining the motorway

**Q523**

When may you stop on a motorway?

*Mark three answers*

- a If you have to read a map
- b When you are tired and need a rest
- c If red lights show above every lane
- d When told to by the police
- e If a child in the car feels ill
- f In an emergency or a breakdown

**Q524**

A crawler lane on a motorway is found

*Mark one answer*

- a on a steep gradient
- b before a service area
- c before a junction
- d along the hard shoulder

**Q525**

After a breakdown you need to rejoin the main carriageway of a motorway from the hard shoulder. You should

*Mark one answer*

- a move out onto the carriageway then build up your speed
- b move out onto the carriageway using your hazard lights
- c gain speed on the hard shoulder before moving out onto the carriageway
- d wait on the hard shoulder until someone flashes their headlights at you

## Q526

Your vehicle has broken down on a motorway. You are not able to stop on the hard shoulder. What should you do?

*Mark one answer*

- ○ a  Switch on your hazard warning lights
- ○ b  Stop following traffic and ask for help
- ○ c  Attempt to repair your vehicle quickly
- ○ d  Place a warning triangle in the road

## Q527

You are allowed to stop on a motorway when you

*Mark one answer*

- ○ a  need to walk and get fresh air
- ○ b  wish to pick up hitch hikers
- ○ c  are told to do so by flashing red lights
- ○ d  need to use a mobile telephone

## Q528

You are driving on a motorway. There are red flashing lights above every lane. You must

*Mark one answer*

- ○ a  pull onto the hard shoulder
- ○ b  slow down and watch for further signals
- ○ c  leave at the next exit
- ○ d  stop and wait

## Q529

You are driving in the right hand lane on a motorway. You see these overhead signs. This means

*Mark one answer*

- ○ a  move to the left and reduce your speed to 50 mph
- ○ b  there are roadworks 50 metres (55 yards) ahead
- ○ c  use the hard shoulder until you have passed the hazard
- ○ d  leave the motorway at the next exit

## Q530

The minimum safe time gap to keep between you and the vehicle in front in good conditions is at least

*Mark one answer*

- ○ a  four seconds
- ○ b  one second
- ○ c  three seconds
- ○ d  two seconds

**Q531**

When driving through a contraflow system on a motorway you should

*Mark one answer*

- ◯ a  ensure that you do not exceed 30 mph for safety
- ◯ b  keep a good distance from the vehicle ahead, for safety
- ◯ c  switch lanes to keep the traffic flowing
- ◯ d  drive close to the vehicle ahead to reduce queues

**Q532**

You are intending to leave the motorway at the next exit. Before you reach the exit you should normally position your vehicle

*Mark one answer*

- ◯ a  in the middle lane
- ◯ b  in the left-hand lane
- ◯ c  on the hard shoulder
- ◯ d  in any lane

**Q533**

What do these motorway signs show?

*Mark one answer*

- ◯ a  They are countdown markers to a bridge
- ◯ b  They are distance markers to the next telephone
- ◯ c  They are countdown markers to the next exit
- ◯ d  They warn of a police control ahead

**Q534**

At night, when leaving a well-lit motorway service area, you should

*Mark one answer*

- ◯ a  drive for some time using only your sidelights
- ◯ b  give your eyes time to adjust to the darkness
- ◯ c  switch on your interior light until your eyes adjust
- ◯ d  close your eyes for a moment before leaving the slip road

## Q535

You are driving on a motorway. By mistake, you go past the exit that you wanted to take. You should

*Mark one answer*

- a carefully reverse on the hard shoulder
- b carry on to the next exit
- c carefully reverse in the left-hand lane
- d make a U-turn at the next gap in the central reservation

## Q536

On a motorway the amber reflective studs can be found between

*Mark one answer*

- a the hard shoulder and the carriageway
- b the acceleration lane and the carriageway
- c the central reservation and the carriageway
- d each pair of the lanes

## Q537

What colour are the reflective studs between a motorway and its slip road?

*Mark one answer*

- a Amber
- b White
- c Green
- d Red

## Q538

What colour are the reflective studs between the lanes on a motorway?

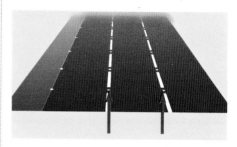

*Mark one answer*

- a Green
- b Amber
- c White
- d Red

## Q539

You are driving on a three-lane motorway. There are red reflective studs on your left and white ones to your right. Where are you?

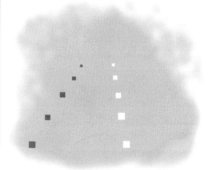

*Mark one answer*

- a In the right-hand lane
- b In the middle lane
- c On the hard shoulder
- d In the left-hand lane

## Answers and Explanations

Q490  b

Q491  c

Q492  a, d, e, f

Q493  d  Speed limits may be altered due to weather conditions. Look out for signs on the central reserve or above your lane.

Q494  d  Check oil and windscreen washer levels and also check the tyres. Plan your rest stops.

Q495  d

Q496  c  You need to build up your speed to that of the traffic already on the motorway so you can ease into a gap in the flow of traffic.

Q497  d

Q498  d

Q499  d

Q500  c  When towing a trailer strong winds can affect stability.

Q501  c

Q502  a  The other lanes should be used for overtaking.

Q503  b

Q504  d  You should always use the left-hand lane for normal driving.

Q505  a  Strictly speaking, any vehicle which is allowed on a motorway.

Q506  b

Q507  d

Q508  b

Q509  c

Q510  d

Q511  d

Q512  a

Q513  b, e

Q514  a

Q515  c

Q516  d, f

Q517  c

Q518  d

Q519  b  It is dangerous to attempt to change the wheel yourself. Try to keep as far from the carriageway as possible whilst waiting for assistance.

Q520  b

Q521  b

Q522  a  You may only stop on the hard shoulder in an emergency.

Q523  c, d, f  Service areas are not officially part of the motorway.

Q524  a

Q525  c

Q526  a

Q527  c

Q528  d

Q529  a

Q530  d  In distance, this gives you one metre per mph of speed. Therefore at 70 mph, using the two-second rule, you would be leaving a gap of 70 metres.

Q531  b  In these circumstances there may also be a speed limit – keep to it.

Q532  b

Q533  c

Q534  b

Q535  b

Q536  c

Q537  c

Q538  c

Q539  d

**Driving Theory Test Questions**

# Roads and Regulations – Other Roads

**Q540**

You may drive over a footpath

*Mark one answer*
- a   to overtake slow-moving traffic
- b   when the pavement is very wide
- c   if no pedestrians are near
- d   to get into a property

**Q541**

What is the meaning of this sign?

*Mark one answer*
- a   Local speed limit applies
- b   No waiting on the carriageway
- c   National speed limit applies
- d   No entry to vehicular traffic

**Q542**

What is the national speed limit on a single carriageway road for cars and motorcycles?

*Mark one answer*
- a   70 mph
- b   60 mph
- c   50 mph
- d   30 mph

**Q543**

What is the national speed limit for cars and motorcycles on a dual carriageway?

*Mark one answer*
- a   30 mph
- b   50 mph
- c   60 mph
- d   70 mph

**Q544**

A single carriageway road has this sign. What is the maximum permitted speed for a car towing a trailer?

*Mark one answer*
- a   30 mph
- b   40 mph
- c   50 mph
- d   60 mph

**Q545**

You are driving along a road that has no traffic signs. There are street lights. What is the speed limit?

*Mark one answer*
- a   20 mph
- b   30 mph
- c   40 mph
- d   60 mph

**Q546**

There are no speed limit signs on the road. How is a 30 mph limit indicated?

*Mark one answer*

- a   By hazard warning lines
- b   By street lighting
- c   By pedestrian islands
- d   By double or single yellow lines

**Q547**

Where you see street lights but no speed limit signs the limit is usually

*Mark one answer*

- a   30 mph
- b   40 mph
- c   50 mph
- d   60 mph

**Q548**

You see this sign ahead of you. It means

*Mark one answer*

- a   start to slow down to 30 mph after passing it
- b   you are leaving the 30 mph speed limit area
- c   do not exceed 30 mph after passing it
- d   the minimum speed limit ahead is 30 mph

**Q549**

If you see a 30 mph limit ahead it means

*Mark one answer*

- a   that the restriction applies only during the working day
- b   that you must not exceed this speed
- c   that it is a guide and you are allowed to drive 10% faster
- d   that you must keep your speed up to 30 mph

**Q550**

What does a speed limit sign like this mean?

*Mark one answer*

- a   It is safe to drive at the speed shown
- b   The speed shown is the advised maximum
- c   The speed shown allows for various road and weather conditions
- d   You must not exceed the speed shown

## Q551

You are towing a small caravan on a dual carriageway. You must not exceed

*Mark one answer*

- a   50 mph
- b   40 mph
- c   70 mph
- d   60 mph

## Q552

What does this sign mean?

*Mark one answer*

- a   Minimum speed 30 mph
- b   End of maximum speed
- c   End of minimum speed
- d   Maximum speed 30 mph

## Q553

You meet an obstruction on your side of the road. You should

*Mark one answer*

- a   drive on; it is your right of way
- b   give way to oncoming traffic
- c   wave oncoming vehicles through
- d   accelerate to get past first

## Q554

You are driving along a street with parked vehicles on the left-hand side. For which THREE reasons should you keep your speed down?

*Mark three answers*

- a   So that oncoming traffic can see you more clearly
- b   You may set off car alarms
- c   Vehicles may be pulling out
- d   Drivers' doors may open
- e   Children may run out from between the vehicles

## Q555

There is a tractor ahead of you. You wish to overtake but you are NOT sure if it is safe to do so. You should

*Mark one answer*

- a   follow another overtaking vehicle through
- b   sound your horn to the slow vehicle to pull over
- c   speed through but flash your lights to oncoming traffic
- d   not overtake if you are in doubt

## Q556

Which three of the following are most likely to take an unusual course at roundabouts?

*Mark three answers*

- a   Horse riders
- b   Milk floats
- c   Delivery vans
- d   Long vehicles
- e   Estate cars
- f   Cyclists

## Q557

You are leaving your vehicle parked on a road. When may you leave the engine running?

*Mark one answer*

- a  If you will be parked for less than five minutes
- b  If the battery is flat
- c  When in a 20 mph zone
- d  Not on any occasion

## Q558

In which FOUR places must you NOT park or wait?

*Mark four answers*

- a  On a dual carriageway
- b  At a bus stop
- c  On the slope of a hill
- d  Opposite a traffic island
- e  In front of someone else's drive
- f  On the brow of a hill

## Q559

What is the nearest you may park your vehicle to a junction?

*Mark one answer*

- a  10 metres (32 feet)
- b  12 metres (39 feet)
- c  15 metres (49 feet)
- d  20 metres (66 feet)

## Q560

You are finding it difficult to find a parking place in a busy town. You can see there is space on the zigzag lines of a zebra crossing. Can you park there?

*Mark one answer*

- a  No, unless you stay with your car
- b  Yes, in order to drop off a passenger
- c  Yes, if you do not block people from crossing
- d  No, not in any circumstances

## Q561

In which TWO places must you NOT park?

*Mark two answers*

- a  Near a school entrance
- b  Near a police station
- c  In a side road
- d  At a bus stop
- e  In a one-way street

## Q562

In which THREE places must you NOT park your vehicle?

*Mark three answers*

- a  Near the brow of a hill
- b  At or near a bus stop
- c  Where there is no pavement
- d  Within 10 metres (32 feet) of a junction
- e  On a 40 mph road

## Q563

On a clearway you must not stop

*Mark one answer*
- a at any time
- b when it is busy
- c in the rush hour
- d during daylight hours

## Q564

You are driving on an urban clearway. You may stop only to

*Mark one answer*
- a set down and pick up passengers
- b use a mobile telephone
- c ask for directions
- d load or unload goods

## Q565

You want to park and you see this sign. On the days and times shown you should

Meter
ZONE

Mon - Fri
8.30 am - 6.30 pm
Saturday
8.30 am - 1.30 pm

*Mark one answer*
- a park in a bay and not pay
- b park on yellow lines and pay
- c park on yellow lines and not pay
- d park in a bay and pay

## Q566

What is the meaning of this sign?

*Mark one answer*
- a No entry
- b Waiting restrictions
- c National speed limit
- d School crossing patrol

## Q567

What MUST you have to park in a disabled space?

DISABLED

*Mark one answer*
- a An orange badge
- b A wheelchair
- c An advanced driver certificate
- d A modified vehicle

**Q568**

You are looking for somewhere to park your vehicle. The area is full EXCEPT for spaces marked 'disabled use'. You can

*Mark one answer*

- a  use these spaces when elsewhere is full
- b  park if you stay with your vehicle
- c  use these spaces, disabled or not
- d  not park there unless permitted

**Q569**

Your vehicle is parked on the road at night. When must you use sidelights?

*Mark one answer*

- a  Where there are continuous white lines in the middle of the road
- b  Where the speed limit exceeds 30 mph
- c  Where you are facing oncoming traffic
- d  Where you are near a bus stop

**Q570**

You park overnight on a road with a 40 mph speed limit. You should

*Mark one answer*

- a  park facing the traffic
- b  park with sidelights on
- c  park with dipped headlights on
- d  park near a street light

**Q571**

You can park on the right-hand side of a road at night

*Mark one answer*

- a  in a one-way street
- b  with your sidelights on
- c  more than 10 metres (32 feet) from a junction
- d  under a lamp-post

**Q572**

On a three-lane dual carriageway the right-hand lane can be used for

*Mark one answer*

- a  overtaking only, never turning right
- b  overtaking or turning right
- c  fast-moving traffic only
- d  turning right only, never overtaking

**Q573**

You are driving at night with full beam headlights on. A vehicle is overtaking you. You should dip your lights

*Mark one answer*

- a  some time after the vehicle has passed you
- b  before the vehicle starts to pass you
- c  only if the other driver dips his headlights
- d  as soon as the vehicle passes you

### Q574

You are driving on a two-lane dual carriageway. For which TWO of the following would you use the right-hand lane?

*Mark two answers*
- ◯ a  Turning right
- ◯ b  Normal driving
- ◯ c  Driving at the minimum allowed speed
- ◯ d  Constant high speed driving
- ◯ e  Overtaking slower traffic
- ◯ f  Mending punctures

### Q575

You are driving in the right-hand lane of a dual carriageway. You see signs showing that the right lane is closed 800 yards ahead. You should

**GET IN LANE**

**800 yards**

*Mark one answer*
- ◯ a  keep in that lane until you reach the queue
- ◯ b  move to the left immediately
- ◯ c  wait and see which lane is moving faster
- ◯ d  move to the left in good time

### Q576

You are entering an area of roadworks. There is a temporary speed limit displayed. You must

*Mark one answer*
- ◯ a  not exceed the speed limit
- ◯ b  obey the limit only during rush hour
- ◯ c  accept the speed limit as advisable
- ◯ d  obey the limit except for overnight

### Q577

While driving, you approach roadworks. You see a temporary maximum speed limit sign. You must

*Mark one answer*
- ◯ a  comply with the sign during the working day
- ◯ b  comply with the sign at all times
- ◯ c  comply with the sign when the lanes are narrow
- ◯ d  comply with the sign during the hours of darkness

### Q578

You may drive a motor car in this bus lane

*Mark one answer*
- ◯ a  outside its operation hours
- ◯ b  to get to the front of a traffic queue
- ◯ c  at no times at all
- ◯ d  to overtake slow moving traffic

## Q579

As a car driver which THREE lanes are you NOT normally allowed to use?

*Mark three answers*

○ a  Crawler lane
○ b  Bus lane
○ c  Overtaking lane
○ d  Acceleration lane
○ e  Cycle lane
○ f  Tram lane

## Q580

You are driving on a road that has a cycle lane. The lane is marked by a broken white line. This means that

*Mark two answers*

○ a  you should not drive in the lane unless it is unavoidable
○ b  you should not park in the lane unless it is unavoidable
○ c  you can drive in the lane at any time
○ d  the lane must be used by motorcyclists in heavy traffic

## Q581

You are driving along a road that has a cycle lane. The lane is marked by a solid white line. This means that during its period of operation

*Mark one answer*

○ a  the lane may be used for parking your car
○ b  you may drive in that lane at any time
○ c  the lane may be used when necessary
○ d  you must not drive in that lane

## Q582

A cycle lane is marked by a solid white line. You must not drive or park in it

*Mark one answer*

○ a  at any time
○ b  during the rush hour
○ c  if a cyclist is using it
○ d  during its period of operation

## Q583

You are approaching a busy junction. There are several lanes with road markings. At the last moment you realise that you are in the wrong lane. You should

*Mark one answer*

○ a  continue in that lane
○ b  force your way across
○ c  stop until the area has cleared
○ d  use clear arm signals to cut across

## Q584

Where may you overtake on a one-way street?

*Mark one answer*

○ a  Only on the left-hand side
○ b  Overtaking is not allowed
○ c  Only on the right-hand side
○ d  Either on the right or the left

**Q585**

You are going along a single-track road with passing places only on the right. The driver behind wishes to overtake. You should

*Mark one answer*

○ a    speed up to get away from the following driver
○ b    switch on your hazard warning lights
○ c    wait opposite a passing place on your right
○ d    drive into a passing place on your right

**Q586**

You are on a road that is only wide enough for one vehicle. There is a car coming towards you. Which TWO of these would be correct?

*Mark two answers*

○ a    Pull into a passing place on your right
○ b    Force the other driver to reverse
○ c    Pull into a passing place if your vehicle is wider
○ d    Pull into a passing place on your left
○ e    Wait opposite a passing place on your right
○ f    Wait opposite a passing place on your left

**Q587**

Signals are normally given by direction indicators and

*Mark one answer*

○ a    brake lights
○ b    side lights
○ c    fog lights
○ d    interior lights

**Q588**

When going straight ahead at a roundabout you should

*Mark one answer*

○ a    indicate left before leaving the roundabout
○ b    not indicate at any time
○ c    indicate right when approaching the roundabout
○ d    indicate left when approaching the roundabout

**Q589**

Which vehicle might have to use a different course to normal at roundabouts?

*Mark one answer*

○ a    Sports car
○ b    Van
○ c    Estate car
○ d    Long vehicle

**Q590**

You are going straight ahead at a roundabout. How should you signal?

*Mark one answer*

○ a    Signal right on the approach and then left to leave the roundabout
○ b    Signal left as you leave the roundabout
○ c    Signal left on the approach to the roundabout and keep the signal on until you leave
○ d    Signal left just after you pass the exit before the one you will take

**Q591**

At a crossroads, there are no signs or road markings. Two vehicles approach. Which has priority?

*Mark one answer*

- a Neither vehicle
- b The vehicle travelling the fastest
- c The vehicle on the widest road
- d Vehicles approaching from the right

**Q592**

Who has priority at an unmarked crossroads?

*Mark one answer*

- a The driver of the larger vehicle
- b No one
- c The driver who is going faster
- d The driver on the wider road

**Q593**

You are intending to turn right at a junction. An oncoming driver is also turning right. It will normally be safer to

*Mark one answer*

- a keep the other vehicle to your RIGHT and turn behind it (offside to offside)
- b keep the other vehicle to your LEFT and turn in front of it (nearside to nearside)
- c carry on and turn at the next junction instead
- d hold back and wait for the other driver to turn first

**Q594**

The dual carriageway you are turning right onto has a narrow central reserve. You should

*Mark one answer*

- a proceed to central reserve and wait
- b wait until the road is clear in both directions
- c stop in first lane so that other vehicles give way
- d emerge slightly to show your intentions

**Q595**

While driving, you intend to turn left into a minor road. On the approach you should

*Mark one answer*

- a keep just left of the middle of the road
- b keep in the middle of the road
- c swing out wide just before turning
- d keep well to the left of the road

**Q596**

You may only enter a box junction when

*Mark one answer*

- a there are less than two vehicles in front of you
- b the traffic lights show green
- c your exit road is clear
- d you need to turn left

## Q597

You may wait in a yellow box junction when

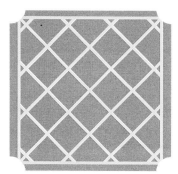

*Mark one answer*

- a  oncoming traffic is preventing you from turning right
- b  you are in a queue of traffic turning left
- c  you are in a queue of traffic to go ahead
- d  you are on a roundabout

## Q598

You want to turn right at a box junction. There is oncoming traffic. You should

*Mark one answer*

- a  wait in the box junction if your exit is clear
- b  wait before the junction until it is clear of all traffic
- c  drive on: you cannot turn right at a box junction
- d  drive slowly into the box junction when signalled by oncoming traffic

## Q599

On which THREE occasions MUST you stop your vehicle?

*Mark three answers*

- a  When involved in an accident
- b  At a red traffic light
- c  When signalled to do so by a police officer
- d  At a junction with double broken white lines
- e  At a pelican crossing when the amber light is flashing and no pedestrians are crossing

## Q600

You MUST stop when signalled to do so by which THREE of these?

*Mark three answers*

- a  A police officer
- b  A pedestrian
- c  A school crossing patrol
- d  A bus driver
- e  A red traffic light

## Q601

At roadworks which of the following can control traffic flow?

*Mark three answers*

- a  A STOP–GO board
- b  Flashing amber lights
- c  A policeman
- d  Flashing red lights
- e  Temporary traffic lights

## Q602

You are waiting at a level crossing. The red warning lights continue to flash after a train has passed by. What should you do?

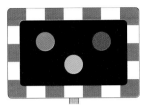

*Mark one answer*

- ○ a   Get out and investigate
- ○ b   Telephone the signal operator
- ○ c   Continue to wait
- ○ d   Drive across carefully

## Q603

You are driving over a level crossing. The warning lights come on and a bell rings. What should you do?

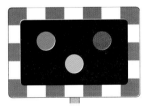

*Mark one answer*

- ○ a   Get everyone out of the vehicle immediately
- ○ b   Stop and reverse back to clear the crossing
- ○ c   Keep going and clear the crossing
- ○ d   Stop immediately and use your hazard warning lights

## Q604

You are waiting at a level crossing. A train has passed but the lights keep flashing. You must

*Mark one answer*

- ○ a   carry on waiting
- ○ b   phone the signal operator
- ○ c   edge over the stop line and look for trains
- ○ d   park your vehicle and investigate

## Q605

You will see these markers when approaching

*Mark one answer*

- ○ a   the end of a motorway
- ○ b   a concealed level crossing
- ○ c   a concealed speed limit sign
- ○ d   the end of a dual carriageway

## Q606

Someone is waiting to cross at a zebra crossing. They are standing on the pavement. You should normally

*Mark one answer*

- ○ a   go on quickly before they step onto the crossing
- ○ b   stop before you reach the zigzag lines and let them cross
- ○ c   stop, let them cross, wait patiently
- ○ d   ignore them as they are still on the pavement

## Q607

At toucan crossings, apart from pedestrians you should be aware of

*Mark one answer*

- ○ a   emergency vehicles emerging
- ○ b   buses pulling out
- ○ c   trams crossing in front
- ○ d   cyclists riding across

## Q608

Who can use a toucan crossing?

*Mark two answers*

- ○ a   Trains
- ○ b   Cyclists
- ○ c   Buses
- ○ d   Pedestrians
- ○ e   Trams

## Q609

At a pelican crossing, what does a flashing amber light mean?

*Mark one answer*

- ○ a   You must not move off until the lights stop flashing
- ○ b   You must give way to pedestrians still on the crossing
- ○ c   You can move off, even if pedestrians are still on the crossing
- ○ d   You must stop because the lights are about to change to red

## Q610

You are waiting at a pelican crossing. The red light changes to flashing amber. This means you must

*Mark one answer*

- ○ a   wait for pedestrians on the crossing to clear
- ○ b   move off immediately without any hesitation
- ○ c   wait for the green light before moving off
- ○ d   get ready and go when the continuous amber light shows

## Q611

You are on a busy main road and find that you are travelling in the wrong direction. What should you do?

*Mark one answer*

- ○ a   Turn into a side road on the right and reverse into the main road
- ○ b   Make a U-turn in the main road
- ○ c   Make a 'three-point' turn in the main road
- ○ d   Turn round in a side road

## Q612

You may remove your seat belt when carrying out a manoeuvre that involves

*Mark one answer*

- ○ a   reversing
- ○ b   a hill start
- ○ c   an emergency stop
- ○ d   driving slowly

## Q613

You are parked in a busy high street. What is the safest way to turn your vehicle around to go the opposite way?

*Mark one answer*

- a   Find a quiet side road to turn round in
- b   Drive into a side road and reverse into the main road
- c   Get someone to stop the traffic
- d   Do a U-turn

## Q614

When you are NOT sure that it is safe to reverse your vehicle you should

*Mark one answer*

- a   use your horn
- b   rev your engine
- c   get out and check
- d   reverse slowly

## Q615

When may you reverse from a side road into a main road?

*Mark one answer*

- a   Only if both roads are clear of traffic
- b   Not at any time
- c   At any time
- d   Only if the main road is clear of traffic

## Q616

You must not reverse

*Mark one answer*

- a   for longer than necessary
- b   for more than a car's length
- c   into a side road
- d   in a built-up area

## Q617

You are reversing your vehicle into a side road. When would the greatest hazard to passing traffic occur?

*Mark one answer*

- a   After you've completed the manoeuvre
- b   Just before you actually begin to manoeuvre
- c   After you've entered the side road
- d   When the front of your vehicle swings out

## Q618

You take the wrong route and find you are on a one-way street. You should

*Mark one answer*

- a   reverse out of the road
- b   turn round in a side road
- c   continue to the end of the road
- d   reverse into a driveway

## Q619

As a provisional licence holder, you must not drive a motor car

*Mark two answers*
- a at more than 50 mph
- b on your own
- c on the motorway
- d under the age of 18 years of age at night
- e with passengers in the rear seats

### Answers and Explanations

Q540  d
Q541  c
Q542  b
Q543  d  The national speed limit is 70 mph on a motorway or dual carriageway and 60 mph on two-way roads unless traffic signs denote anything different.
Q544  c
Q545  b  If there are street lights, the speed limit is 30 mph unless a road sign states otherwise.
Q546  b
Q547  a  If there is any difference there would be repeated signs on the light posts.
Q548  c  You should adjust your speed so that you are travelling at no more than 30 mph as you pass the sign.
Q549  b
Q550  d  This sign gives an order which tells you the maximum speed at which you are allowed to drive. It is a law, not a piece of advice, and does not in any way imply that it will always be safe to drive at that speed.
Q551  d
Q552  c
Q553  b
Q554  c, d, e
Q555  d
Q556  a, d, f
Q557  d
Q558  b, d, e, f
Q559  a
Q560  d  It is illegal to park on the zig-zag lines of a pedestrian crossing for any reason or at any time.
Q561  a, d
Q562  a, b, d
Q563  a
Q564  a
Q565  d
Q566  b
Q567  a
Q568  d
Q569  b  You are not allowed to park at 'a' or 'd' at any time; 'c' is wrong because you must park on the left at night unless in a one-way street.
Q570  b
Q571  a
Q572  b
Q573  d  If you dip your lights too early you may reduce your vision; too late and you may dazzle the driver who has overtaken.
Q574  a, e
Q575  d
Q576  a
Q577  b
Q578  a
Q579  b, e, f
Q580  a, b

Q581  d

Q582  d

Q583  a  All the other actions suggested could be dangerous.

Q584  d

Q585  c

Q586  d, e

Q587  a  When you press your brake pedal the brake lights come on, warning other vehicles behind.

Q588  a  You should signal left just as you pass the exit before the one you want to take.

Q589  d

Q590  d  This is correct for most roundabouts. Bear in mind that some roundabouts do not have an exit to the left, so the first exit is straight ahead.

Q591  a  You often find these on housing estates. Approach with caution and be prepared to give way.

Q592  b  An unmarked crossroads has no road signs or road markings and no vehicle has priority even if one road is wider or busier than the other.

Q593  a

Q594  b  Because the central reserve is narrow, you would partly block the road if you drove to the middle and had to wait.

Q595  d

Q596  c

Q597  a

Q598  a

Q599  a, b, c  'd' is wrong because although the double, broken white lines at a junction mean 'give way', you do not necessarily have to stop in order to do so. 'e' is wrong because you may drive on at a pelican crossing when the amber light is flashing if no pedestrians are crossing.

Q600  a, c, e  Note the word 'MUST' in the question, which is asking what the law says.

Q601  a, c, e

Q602  c  You should wait for three minutes. If no further train passes you should telephone the signal operator.

Q603  c  You are already on the crossing when the warning lights come on, so 'c' is correct.

Q604  a

Q605  b  These countdown markers indicate the distance to the stop line at the concealed level crossing.

Q606  c  Note the word 'normally'. You should give way if safe to do so.

Q607  d  Cyclists are allowed to ride across toucan crossings, unlike other crossings where they must dismount.

Q608  b, d  Toucan crossings are shared by pedestrians and cyclists together.

Q609  b  You may drive as soon as the crossing is clear and before the flashing amber light changes to green.

Q610  a

Q611  d  It is illegal to reverse from a minor to a major road, so 'a' is wrong. 'b' and 'c' would be dangerous because the road is busy.

Q612  a

Q613  a
Q614  c
Q615  b
Q616  a
Q617  d  Always remember to check all
          round just before steering and
          give way to any road users.
Q618  c
Q619  b, c

**Driving Theory Test Questions**

# Signs and Signals

## Q620

You MUST obey signs giving orders. These signs are mostly in

*Mark one answer*

- a  green rectangles
- b  red triangles
- c  blue rectangles
- ✗ d  red circles

## Q621

Traffic signs giving orders are generally which shape?

*Mark one answer*

○ a                    ○ b

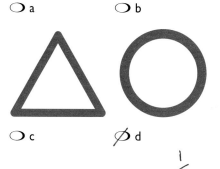

○ c                    ✗ d

## Q622

Which type of sign tells you NOT to do something?

*Mark one answer*

○ a                    ○ b

✗ c                    ○ d

## Q623

What does this sign mean?

*Mark one answer*

- ✗ a  Maximum speed limit with traffic calming
- b  Minimum speed limit with traffic calming
- c  20 cars only parking zone
- d  Only 20 cars allowed at any one time

## Q624

Which sign means no motor vehicles are allowed?

*Mark one answer*

○ a        ⊘ b

✗ c        ○ d

## Q626

Which of these signs means no motor vehicles?

*Mark one answer*

⊘ a        ✗ b

○ c        ○ d

## Q625

What does this sign mean?

*Mark one answer*

○ a    New speed limit 20 mph
○ b    No vehicles over 30 tonnes
○ c    Minimum speed limit 30 mph
⊘ d    End of 20 mph zone

## Q627

This traffic sign means there is

*Mark one answer*

⊘ a    a compulsory maximum speed limit
○ b    an advised maximum speed limit
○ c    a compulsory minimum speed limit
○ d    an advised separation distance

## Q628

What does this sign mean?

*Mark one answer*
- ○ a No overtaking
- ⊘ b No motor vehicles
- ○ c Clearway (no stopping)
- ○ d Cars and motorcycles only

## Q629

What does this sign mean?

*Mark one answer*
- ○ a No parking
- ○ b No road markings
- ○ c No through road
- ⊘ d No entry

## Q630

What does this sign mean?

*Mark one answer*
- ○ a Bend to the right
- ○ b Road on the right closed
- ○ c No traffic from the right
- ⊘ d No right turn

## Q631

Which sign means 'no entry'?

*Mark one answer*

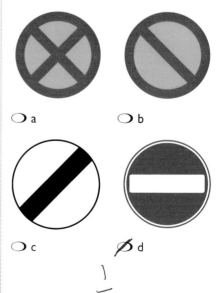

- ○ a
- ○ b
- ○ c
- ⊘ d

## Q632

What does this sign mean?

*Mark one answer*

- ✗ a   Route for trams only
- ○ b   Route for buses only
- ○ c   Parking for buses only
- ○ d   Parking for trams only

## Q633

Which type of vehicle does this sign apply to?

*Mark one answer*

- ○ a   Wide vehicles
- ○ b   Long vehicles
- ✗ c   High vehicles
- ○ d   Heavy vehicles

## Q634

Which sign means NO motor vehicles allowed?

*Mark one answer*

○ a        ✗ b

○ c        ○ d

## Q635

What does this sign mean?

*Mark one answer*

- ○ a   You have priority
- ○ b   No motor vehicles
- ○ c   Two-way traffic
- ✗ d   No overtaking

## Q636

What does this sign mean?

*Mark one answer*

- a  Keep in one lane
- b  Give way to oncoming traffic
- c  Do not overtake
- d  Form two lanes

## Q637

Which sign means no overtaking?

*Mark one answer*

- a
- b
- c
- d

## Q638

What does this sign mean?

*Mark one answer*

- a  Waiting restrictions apply
- b  Waiting permitted
- c  National speed limit applies
- d  Clearway (no stopping)

## Q639

What does this sign mean?

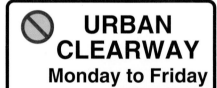

*Mark one answer*

- a  You can park on the days and times shown
- b  No parking on the days and times shown
- c  No parking at all from Monday to Friday
- d  You can park at any time; the urban clearway ends

## Q640

What does this sign mean?

*Mark one answer*

- a   End of restricted speed area
- b   End of restricted parking area
- c   End of clearway
- d   End of cycle route

## Q641

Which sign means 'no stopping'?

*Mark one answer*

a

b

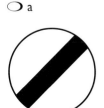

c

d

## Q642

What does this sign mean?

*Mark one answer*

- a   Roundabout
- b   Crossroads
- c   No stopping
- d   No entry

## Q643

You see this sign ahead. It means

*Mark one answer*

- a   national speed limit applies
- b   waiting restrictions apply
- c   no stopping
- d   no entry

## Q644

What does this sign mean?

Mark one answer
- ☒ a   Distance to parking place ahead
- ◯ b   Distance to public telephone ahead
- ◯ c   Distance to public house ahead
- ☒ d   Distance to passing place ahead

## Q645

What does this sign mean?

Mark one answer
- ◯ a   Vehicles may not park on the verge or footway
- ◯ b   Vehicles may park on the left-hand side of the road only
- ☒ c   Vehicles may park fully on the verge or footway
- ◯ d   Vehicles may park on the right-hand side of the road only

## Q646

What does this traffic sign mean?

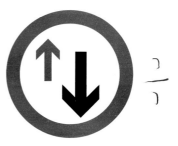

Mark one answer
- ◯ a   No overtaking allowed
- ☒ b   Give priority to oncoming traffic
- ◯ c   Two-way traffic
- ◯ d   One-way traffic only

## Q647

What is the meaning of this traffic sign?

Mark one answer
- ◯ a   End of two-way road
- ☒ b   Give priority to vehicles coming towards you
- ◯ c   You have priority over vehicles coming towards you
- ◯ d   Bus lane ahead

## Q648

Which sign means 'traffic has priority over oncoming vehicles'?

*Mark one answer*

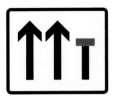
○ a

○ b

✖ c

✖ d

## Q649

What MUST you do when you see this sign?

*Mark one answer*
- ○ a Stop, ONLY if traffic is approaching
- ✖ b Stop, even if the road is clear
- ○ c Stop, ONLY if children are waiting to cross
- ○ d Stop, ONLY if a red light is showing

## Q650

What does this sign mean?

*Mark one answer*
- ○ a No overtaking
- ○ b You are entering a one-way street
- ○ c Two-way traffic ahead
- ✖ d You have priority over vehicles from the opposite direction

## Q651

What shape is a STOP sign at a junction?

*Mark one answer*

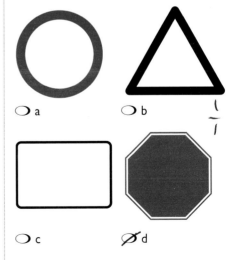
○ a          ○ b

○ c          ✖ d

$\frac{29}{36}$

### Q652

At a junction you see this sign partly covered by snow. What does it mean?

$\frac{1}{1}$

*Mark one answer*

- a  Crossroads
- b  Give way
- c  Stop
- d  Turn right

### Q653

Which shape is used for a GIVE WAY sign?

*Mark one answer*

- a
- b $\frac{0}{1}$
- c
- d

### Q654

What does this sign mean?

$\frac{0}{1}$

*Mark one answer*

- a  Service area 30 miles ahead
- b  Maximum speed 30 mph
- c  Minimum speed 30 mph
- d  Lay-by 30 miles ahead

### Q655

Which of these signs means turn left ahead?

*Mark one answer*

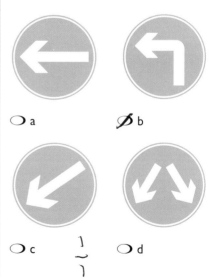

- a
- b
- c $\frac{1}{1}$
- d

## Q656

At a mini-roundabout you should

*Mark one answer*
- a give way to traffic from the right
- b give way to traffic from the left
- c give way to traffic from the other way
- d stop even when clear

## Q657

What does this sign mean?

*Mark one answer*
- a Buses turning
- b Ring road
- c Mini roundabout
- d Keep right

## Q658

What does this sign mean?

*Mark one answer*
- a Give way to oncoming vehicles
- b Approaching traffic passes you on both sides
- c Turn off at the next available junction
- d Pass either side to get to the same destination

## Q659

What does this sign mean?

*Mark one answer*
- a Route for trams
- b Give way to trams
- c Route for buses
- d Give way to buses

## Q660

What does a circular traffic sign with a blue background do?

*Mark one answer*
- a   Give warning of a motorway ahead
- b   Give directions to a car park
- c   Give motorway information
- d   Give an instruction

## Q661

Which of these signs means that you are entering a one-way street?

*Mark one answer*

- a

- b

- c

- d

## Q662

Where would you see a contraflow bus and cycle lane?

*Mark one answer*
- a   On a dual carriageway
- b   On a roundabout
- c   On an urban motorway
- d   On a one-way street

## Q663

What does this sign mean?

*Mark one answer*
- a   Bus station on the right
- b   Contraflow bus lane
- c   With-flow bus lane
- d   Give way to buses

## Q664

What does this sign mean?

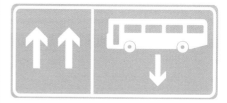

*Mark one answer*
- a   With-flow bus and cycle lane
- b   Contraflow bus and cycle lane
- c   No buses and cycles allowed
- d   No waiting for buses and cycles

## Q665

What does a sign with a brown background show?

*Mark one answer*
- a   Tourist directions
- b   Primary roads
- c   Motorway routes
- d   Minor routes

## Q666

This sign means

*Mark one answer*
- a   tourist attraction
- b   beware of trains
- c   level crossing
- d   beware of trams

## Q667

What are triangular signs for?

*Mark one answer*
- a   To give warnings
- b   To give information
- c   To give orders
- d   To give directions

## Q668

What does this sign mean?

*Mark one answer*
- a   Turn left ahead
- b   T-junction
- c   No through road
- d   Give way

## Q669

What does this sign mean?

*Mark one answer*
- a   Multi-exit roundabout
- b   Risk of ice
- c   Six roads converge
- d   Place of historical interest

## Q670

What does this sign mean?

*Mark one answer*

- ○ a  Crossroads
- ○ b  Level crossing with gate
- ○ c  Level crossing without gate
- ○ d  Ahead only

## Q671

What does this sign mean?

*Mark one answer*

- ○ a  Ring road
- ○ b  Mini-roundabout
- ○ c  No vehicles
- ○ d  Roundabout

## Q672

Which FOUR of these would be indicated by a triangular road sign?

*Mark four answers*

- ○ a  Road narrows
- ○ b  Ahead only
- ○ c  Low bridge
- ○ d  Minimum speed
- ○ e  Children crossing
- ○ f  T-junction

## Q673

What does this sign mean?

*Mark one answer*

- ○ a  Cyclists must dismount
- ○ b  Cycles are not allowed
- ○ c  Cycle route ahead
- ○ d  Cycle in single file

## Q674

Which sign means that pedestrians may be walking along the road?

*Mark one answer*

 a

 b

 c

 d

## Q675

Which of these signs warn you of a pedestrian crossing?

*Mark one answer*

 a

 b

 c

 d

## Q676

What does this sign mean?

*Mark one answer*
- a   No footpath ahead
- b   Pedestrians only ahead
- c   Pedestrian crossing ahead
- d   School crossing ahead

## Q677

What does this sign mean?

*Mark one answer*
- a   School crossing patrol
- b   No pedestrians allowed
- c   Pedestrian zone – no vehicles
- d   Pedestrian crossing ahead

## Q678

Which of these signs means there is a double bend ahead?

*Mark one answer*

○ a        ○ b

○ c        ○ d

## Q679

What does this sign mean?

*Mark one answer*
- ○ a   Wait at the barriers
- ○ b   Wait at the crossroads
- ○ c   Give way to trams
- ○ d   Give way to farm vehicles

## Q680

What does this sign mean?

*Mark one answer*
- ○ a   Humpback bridge
- ○ b   Humps in the road
- ○ c   Entrance to tunnel
- ○ d   Soft verges

## Q681

What does this sign mean?

*Mark one answer*
- ○ a   Low bridge ahead
- ○ b   Tunnel ahead
- ○ c   Ancient monument ahead
- ○ d   Accident black spot ahead

## Q682

What does this sign mean?

*Mark one answer*

- a Two-way traffic straight ahead
- b Two-way traffic crossing a one-way street
- c Two-way traffic over a bridge
- d Two-way traffic crosses a two-way road

## Q683

Which sign means 'two-way traffic crosses a one-way road'?

*Mark one answer*

- a

- b

- c

- d

## Q684

Which of these signs means the end of a dual carriageway?

*Mark one answer*

- a

- b

- c

- d

## Q685

What does this sign mean?

*Mark one answer*

- a End of dual carriageway
- b Tall bridge
- c Road narrows
- d End of narrow bridge

**Q686**

What does this sign mean?

*Mark one answer*

○ a   Two-way traffic ahead across a one-way street
○ b   Traffic approaching you has priority
○ c   Two-way traffic straight ahead
○ d   Motorway contraflow system ahead

**Q687**

What does this sign mean?

*Mark one answer*

○ a   Crosswinds
○ b   Road noise
○ c   Airport
○ d   Adverse camber

**Q688**

What does this traffic sign mean?

*Mark one answer*

○ a   Slippery road ahead
○ b   Tyres liable to punctures ahead
○ c   Danger ahead
○ d   Service area ahead

**Q689**

You are about to overtake when you see this sign. You should

**Hidden dip**

*Mark one answer*

○ a   overtake the other driver as quickly as possible
○ b   move to the right to get a better view
○ c   switch your headlights on before overtaking
○ d   hold back until you can see clearly ahead

### Q690

What does this sign mean?

*Mark one answer*
- a Level crossing with gate or barrier
- b Gated road ahead
- c Level crossing without gate or barrier
- d Cattle grid ahead

### Q691

What does this sign mean?

*Mark one answer*
- a No trams ahead
- b Oncoming trams
- c Trams crossing ahead
- d Trams only

### Q692

What does this sign mean?

*Mark one answer*
- a Adverse camber
- b Steep hill downwards
- c Uneven road
- d Steep hill upwards

### Q693

What does this sign mean?

*Mark one answer*
- a Quayside or river bank
- b Steep hill downwards
- c Slippery road
- d Road liable to flooding

### Q694

What does this sign mean?

*Mark one answer*
- a Uneven road surface
- b Bridge over the road
- c Road ahead ends
- d Water across the road

## Q695

What does this sign mean?

*Mark one answer*

- a   Humpback bridge
- b   Traffic calming hump
- c   Low bridge
- d   Uneven road

## Q696

What does this sign mean?

*Mark one answer*

- a   Turn left for parking area
- b   No through road on the left
- c   No entry for traffic turning left
- d   Turn left for ferry terminal

## Q697

What does this sign mean?

*Mark one answer*

- a   T-junction
- b   No through road
- c   Telephone box ahead
- d   Toilet ahead

## Q698

Which sign means 'no through road'?

*Mark one answer*

a

b

c

d

## Q699

Which of the following signs informs you that you are coming to a No Through Road?

*Mark one answer*

○ a

○ b

○ c

○ d

## Q700

What does this sign mean?

*Mark one answer*

○ a  Direction to park and ride car park
○ b  No parking for buses or coaches
○ c  Directions to bus and coach park
○ d  Parking area for cars and coaches

## Q701

You are driving through a tunnel and you see this sign. What does it mean?

*Mark one answer*

○ a  Direction to emergency pedestrian exit
○ b  Beware of pedestrians, no footpath ahead
○ c  No access for pedestrians
○ d  Beware of pedestrians crossing ahead

## Q702

Which is the sign for a ring road?

*Mark one answer*

○ a

○ b

○ c

○ d

### Q703

What does this sign mean?

*Mark one answer*

○ a   Route for lorries
○ b   Ring road
○ c   Rest area
○ d   Roundabout

### Q704

What does this sign mean?

*Mark one answer*

○ a   Hilly road
○ b   Humps in road
○ c   Holiday route
○ d   Hospital route

### Q705

What does this sign mean?

*Mark one answer*

○ a   The right-hand lane ahead
        is narrow
○ b   Right-hand lane for buses only
○ c   Right-hand lane for turning right
○ d   The right-hand lane is closed

### Q706

What does this sign mean?

*Mark one answer*

○ a   Change to the left lane
○ b   Leave at the next exit
○ c   Contraflow system
○ d   One-way street

## Q707

To avoid an accident when entering a contraflow system, you should

*Mark three answers*

- ○ a reduce speed in good time
- ○ b switch lanes anytime to make progress
- ○ c choose an appropriate lane early
- ○ d keep the correct separation distance
- ○ e increase speed to pass through quickly
- ○ f follow other motorists closely to avoid long queues

## Q708

What does this sign mean?

*Mark one answer*

- ○ a Leave motorway at next exit
- ○ b Lane for heavy and slow vehicles
- ○ c All lorries use the hard shoulder
- ○ d Rest area for lorries

## Q709

You see this traffic light ahead. Which light(s) will come on next?

*Mark one answer*

- ○ a Red alone
- ○ b Red and amber together
- ○ c Green and amber together
- ○ d Green alone

## Q710

You are approaching a red traffic light. The signal will change from red to

*Mark one answer*

- ○ a red and amber, then green
- ○ b green, then amber
- ○ c amber, then green
- ○ d green and amber, then green

**Q711**

A red traffic light means

*Mark one answer*
- a you should stop unless turning left
- b stop, if you are able to brake safely
- c you must stop and wait behind the stop line
- d proceed with caution

**Q712**

At traffic lights, amber on its own means

*Mark one answer*
- a prepare to go
- b go if the way is clear
- c go if no pedestrians are crossing
- d stop at the stop line

**Q713**

A red traffic light means

*Mark one answer*
- a you must stop behind the white stop line
- b you may drive straight on if there is no other traffic
- c you may turn left if it is safe to do so
- d you must slow down and prepare to stop if traffic has started to cross

**Q714**

You are approaching traffic lights. Red and amber are showing. This means

*Mark one answer*
- a pass the lights if the road is clear
- b there is a fault with the lights – take care
- c wait for the green light before you pass the lights
- d the lights are about to change to red

## Q715

You are at a junction controlled by traffic lights. When should you NOT proceed at green?

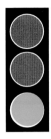

*Mark one answer*

- a When pedestrians are waiting to cross
- b When your exit from the junction is blocked
- c When you think the lights may be about to change
- d When you intend to turn right

## Q716

You are in the left-hand lane at traffic lights. You are waiting to turn left. At which of these traffic lights must you NOT move on?

*Mark one answer*

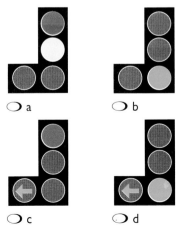

- a
- b
- c
- d

## Q717

What does this sign mean?

*Mark one answer*

- a Traffic lights out of order
- b Amber signal out of order
- c Temporary traffic lights ahead
- d New traffic lights ahead

## Q718

You see this sign at a crossroads. You should

*Mark one answer*

- a maintain the same speed
- b drive on with great care
- c find another route
- d telephone the police

## Q719

When traffic lights are out of order, who has priority?

*Mark one answer*

- a Traffic going straight on
- b Traffic turning right
- c Nobody
- d Traffic turning left

## Q720

These flashing red lights mean STOP.
In which THREE of the following places
could you find them?

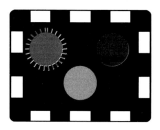

*Mark three answers*

- a   Pelican crossings
- b   Lifting bridges
- c   Zebra crossings
- d   Level crossings
- e   Motorway exits
- f   Fire stations

## Q721

What do these zigzag lines at pedestrian
crossings mean?

*Mark one answer*

- a   No parking at any time
- b   Parking allowed only for a short time
- c   Slow down to 20 mph
- d   Sounding horns is not allowed

## Q722

You are approaching a zebra crossing
where pedestrians are waiting. Which arm
signal might you give?

*Mark one answer*

- a                  - b

- c                  - d

## Q723

The white line along the side of the road

*Mark one answer*

- a   shows the edge of the carriageway
- b   shows the approach to a hazard
- c   means no parking
- d   means no overtaking

## Q724

The white line painted in the centre of the road means

*Mark one answer*

- a   the area is hazardous and you must not overtake
- b   you should give priority to oncoming vehicles
- c   do not cross the line unless the road ahead is clear
- d   the area is a national speed limit zone

## Q725

When may you cross a double solid white line in the middle of the road?

*Mark one answer*

- a   To pass traffic that is queuing back at a junction
- b   To pass a car signalling to turn left ahead
- c   To pass a road maintenance vehicle travelling at 10 mph or less
- d   To pass a vehicle that is towing a trailer

## Q726

A white line like this along the centre of the road is a

*Mark one answer*

- a   bus lane marking
- b   hazard warning
- c   'give way' marking
- d   lane marking

## Q727

You see this white arrow on the road ahead. It means

*Mark one answer*

- a   entrance on the left
- b   all vehicles turn left
- c   keep left of the hatched markings
- d   road bending to the left

## Q728

What does this road marking mean?

*Mark one answer*

- a  Do not cross the line
- b  No stopping allowed
- c  You are approaching a hazard
- d  No overtaking allowed

## Q729

This marking appears on the road just before a

*Mark one answer*

- a  no entry sign
- b  give way sign
- c  stop sign
- d  no through road sign

## Q730

Where would you see this road marking?

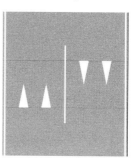

*Mark one answer*

- a  At traffic lights
- b  On road humps
- c  Near a level crossing
- d  At a box junction

## Q731

Which is a hazard warning line?

*Mark one answer*

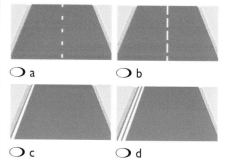

- a
- b
- c
- d

## Q732

You see this line across the road at the entrance to a roundabout. What does it mean?

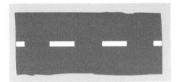

*Mark one answer*
- a  Give way to traffic from the right
- b  Traffic from the left has right of way
- c  You have right of way
- d  Stop at the line

## Q733

At this junction there is a stop sign with a solid white line on the road surface. Why is there a stop sign here?

*Mark one answer*
- a  Speed on the major road is de-restricted
- b  It is a busy junction
- c  Visibility along the major road is restricted
- d  There are hazard warning lines in the centre of the road

## Q734

Where would you find this road marking?

*Mark one answer*
- a  At a railway crossing
- b  At a junction
- c  On a motorway
- d  On a pedestrian crossing

## Q735

How will a police officer in a patrol vehicle normally get you to stop?

*Mark one answer*
- a  Flash the headlights, indicate left and point to the left
- b  Wait until you stop, then approach you
- c  Use the siren, overtake, cut in front and stop
- d  Pull alongside you, use the siren and wave you to stop

## Q736

There is a police car following you. The police officer flashes the headlights and points to the left. What should you do?

*Mark one answer*
- a  Turn at the next left
- b  Pull up on the left
- c  Stop immediately
- d  Move over to the left

## Q737

You approach a junction. The traffic lights are not working. A police officer gives this signal. You should

*Mark one answer*

- ○ a   turn left only
- ○ b   turn right only
- ○ c   stop level with the officer's arm
- ○ d   stop at the stop line

## Q738

The driver of the car in front is giving this arm signal. What does it mean?

*Mark one answer*

- ○ a   The driver is slowing down
- ○ b   The driver intends to turn right
- ○ c   The driver wishes to overtake
- ○ d   The driver intends to turn left

## Q739

The driver of this car is giving an arm signal. What is he about to do?

*Mark one answer*

- ○ a   Turn to the right
- ○ b   Turn to the left
- ○ c   Go straight ahead
- ○ d   Let pedestrians cross

## Q740

Which arm signal tells a following vehicle that you intend to turn left?

*Mark one answer*

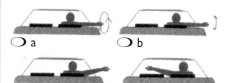

- ○ a            ○ b

- ○ c            ○ d

## Q741

How should you give an arm signal to turn left?

*Mark one answer*

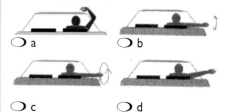

- ○ a            ○ b

- ○ c            ○ d

## Q742

You are signalling to turn right in busy traffic. How would you confirm your intention safely?

*Mark one answer*
- a  Sound the horn
- b  Give an arm signal
- c  Flash your headlamp
- d  Position over the centre line

## Q743

You want to turn right at a junction but you think that your indicators cannot be seen clearly. What should you do?

*Mark one answer*
- a  Get out and check if your indicators can be seen
- b  Stay in the left-hand lane
- c  Keep well over to the right
- d  Give an arm signal as well as an indicator signal

## Q744

When may you sound the horn on your vehicle?

*Mark one answer*
- a  To give you right of way
- b  To attract a friend's attention
- c  To warn others of your presence
- d  To make slower drivers move over

## Q745

You must not use your horn when your vehicle is stationary

*Mark one answer*
- a  unless a moving vehicle may cause you danger
- b  at any time whatsoever
- c  unless it is used only briefly
- d  except for signalling that you have just arrived

## Q746

When motorists flash their headlights at you it means

*Mark one answer*
- a  that there is a radar speed trap ahead
- b  that they are giving way to you
- c  that they are warning you of their presence
- d  that there is something wrong with your vehicle

## Q747

Why should you make sure that you have cancelled your indicators after turning?

*Mark one answer*
- a  To avoid flattening the battery
- b  To avoid misleading other road users
- c  To avoid dazzling other road users
- d  To avoid damage to the indicator relay

## Q748

You are waiting at a T-junction. A vehicle is coming from the right with the left signal flashing. What should you do?

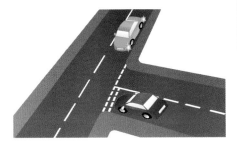

*Mark one answer*

- a   Move out and accelerate hard
- b   Wait until the vehicle starts to turn in
- c   Pull out before the vehicle reaches the junction
- d   Move out slowly

## Q749

When may you use hazard warning lights when driving?

*Mark one answer*

- a   Instead of sounding the horn in a built-up area between 11.30 pm and 7 am
- b   On a motorway or unrestricted dual carriageway, to warn of a hazard ahead
- c   On rural routes, after a warning sign of animals
- d   On the approach to toucan crossings where cyclists are waiting to cross

## Q750

Where would you see these road markings?

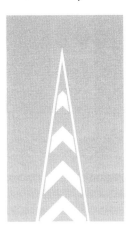

*Mark one answer*

- a   At a level crossing
- b   On a motorway slip road
- c   At a pedestrian crossing
- d   On a single-track road

## Q751

When may you NOT overtake on the left?

*Mark one answer*

- a   On a free-flowing motorway or dual carriageway
- b   When the traffic is moving slowly in queues
- c   On a one-way street
- d   When the car in front is signalling to turn right

## Q752

You are driving on a motorway. There is a slow-moving vehicle ahead. On the back you see this sign. You should

*Mark one answer*

- a   pass on the right
- b   pass on the left
- c   leave at the next exit
- d   drive no further

## Q753

What does this motorway sign mean?

*Mark one answer*

- a   Change to the lane on your left
- b   Leave the motorway at the next exit
- c   Change to the opposite carriageway
- d   Pull up on the hard shoulder

## Q754

What does this motorway sign mean?

*Mark one answer*

- a   Temporary minimum speed 50 mph
- b   No services for 50 miles
- c   Obstruction 50 metres (164 feet) ahead
- d   Temporary maximum speed 50 mph

## Q755

What does this sign mean?

*Mark one answer*

- a   Through traffic to use left lane
- b   Right-hand lane T-junction only
- c   Right-hand lane closed ahead
- d   11 tonne weight limit

**Q756**

On a motorway this sign means

*Mark one answer*
- a   move over onto the hard shoulder
- b   overtaking on the left only
- c   leave the motorway at the next exit
- d   move to the lane on your left

**Q757**

What does '25' mean on this motorway sign?

*Mark one answer*
- a   The distance to the nearest town
- b   The route number of the road
- c   The number of the next junction
- d   The speed limit on the slip road

**Q758**

You are driving on a motorway. Red flashing lights appear above your lane only. What should you do?

*Mark one answer*
- a   Continue in that lane and await further information
- b   Go no further in that lane
- c   Drive onto the hard shoulder
- d   Stop and wait for an instruction to proceed

**Q759**

The right-hand lane of a three-lane motorway is

*Mark one answer*
- a   for lorries only
- b   an overtaking lane
- c   the right-turn lane
- d   an acceleration lane

**Q760**

Where can you find reflective amber studs on a motorway?

*Mark one answer*
- a   Separating the slip road from the motorway
- b   On the left-hand edge of the road
- c   On the right-hand edge of the road
- d   Separating the lanes

## Q761

Where on a motorway would you find green reflective studs?

*Mark one answer*

- a    Separating driving lanes
- b    Between the hard shoulder and the carriageway
- c    At slip road entrances and exits
- d    Between the carriageway and the central reservation

## Q762

You are travelling along a motorway. You see this sign. You should

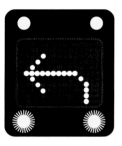

*Mark one answer*

- a    leave the motorway at the next exit
- b    turn left immediately
- c    change lane
- d    move onto the hard shoulder

## Q763

You see these signs overhead on the motorway. They mean

*Mark one answer*

- a    leave the motorway at the next exit
- b    all vehicles use the hard shoulder
- c    sharp bend to the left ahead
- d    stop, all lanes ahead closed

## Q764

What does this sign mean?

*Mark one answer*

- a    No motor vehicles
- b    End of motorway
- c    No through road
- d    End of bus lane

**Q765**

Which of these signs means that the national speed limit applies?

*Mark one answer*

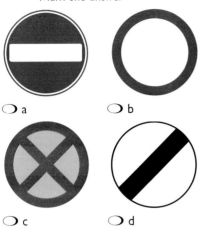

◯ a

◯ b

◯ c

◯ d

**Q766**

What is the maximum speed on a single carriageway road?

*Mark one answer*
◯ a   50 mph
◯ b   60 mph
◯ c   40 mph
◯ d   70 mph

## Answers and Explanations

Q620   d
Q621   d
Q622   a   Red circles tell you what you must not do. Rectangles usually give you information.
Q623   a

Q624   b   This sign means no vehicles except bicycles being pushed by hand.
Q625   d
Q626   a
Q627   a
Q628   b
Q629   d
Q630   d
Q631   d
Q632   a
Q633   c
Q634   b
Q635   d
Q636   c
Q637   b
Q638   a   There will also be a plate indicating when the restriction applies.
Q639   b
Q640   b
Q641   b
Q642   c
Q643   c   This is a clearway sign and you must not stop at all.
Q644   a
Q645   c
Q646   b
Q647   c
Q648   c
Q649   b   You must always stop at a stop sign.
Q650   d
Q651   d
Q652   c
Q653   d
Q654   c
Q655   b
Q656   a
Q657   c
Q658   d

Q659 a

Q660 d Circular signs with blue backgrounds tell you what you must do.

Q661 b

Q662 d

Q663 b

Q664 a

Q665 a

Q666 a

Q667 a

Q668 b

Q669 b

Q670 a

Q671 d

Q672 a, c, e, f

Q673 c

Q674 a

Q675 c

Q676 c

Q677 d

Q678 b

Q679 c

Q680 b

Q681 b Red triangles usually give a warning.

Q682 b

Q683 b

Q684 d

Q685 a

Q686 c

Q687 a

Q688 c

Q689 d The sign is warning of a possible danger ahead so it would be dangerous to overtake.

Q690 a

Q691 c

Q692 b

Q693 a

Q694 d

Q695 a

Q696 b

Q697 b

Q698 c

Q699 c

Q700 a

Q701 a

Q702 c

Q703 b

Q704 c

Q705 d

Q706 c

Q707 a, c, d

Q708 b

Q709 a

Q710 a The sequence of traffic lights is red, then red and amber, then green, then amber alone, then red.

Q711 c You must always stop at a red traffic light.

Q712 d An amber light means stop, and the lights will next change to red.

Q713 a

Q714 c The next light will be green and you must wait to drive on until it appears.

Q715 b

Q716 a

Q717 a

Q718 b

Q719 c

Q720 b, d, f

Q721 a

Q722 a

Q723 a

Q724 c

Q725 c

Q726 b

Q727 c

Q728  c
Q729  b
Q730  b
Q731  b  Long lines with short gaps between them in the middle of the road are hazard warning lines. The more paint the more danger.
Q732  a
Q733  c  Because the major road is on a bend, your vision is restricted to both left and right.
Q734  b
Q735  a
Q736  b  You must stop, but 'c' is wrong because it may not be safe to stop immediately.
Q737  d
Q738  d
Q739  b
Q740  a
Q741  c
Q742  b
Q743  d  Then park in a safe place and check your indicators.
Q744  c  Sounding your horn has the same meaning as flashing your headlights – to warn of your presence.
Q745  a
Q746  c  'c' is the correct answer because that is what flashing your headlights is supposed to mean. Not everyone knows or obeys the rules and may flash their headlights for other reasons, so always try to make sure of what they mean before you decide on any action.
Q747  b
Q748  b  The approaching vehicle might

have left the signal on by mistake, or intended to stop after the junction. Always wait long enough to be sure the vehicle is really turning left.
Q749  b  Note that the question states 'when driving'. The types of roads in 'b' are the only places where it is legal to use hazard warning lights while your car is moving.
Q750  b
Q751  a  You must not overtake on the left on a motorway or dual carriageway unless you are moving in queues of slow-moving traffic.
Q752  b
Q753  a  Obviously you must make sure it is safe before doing so.
Q754  d
Q755  c  Always look well ahead and you will have plenty of time to react.
Q756  d  You must go no further in that lane. You may change lanes and proceed, unless flashing red lights appear above all of them.
Q757  c
Q758  b
Q759  b
Q760  c
Q761  c
Q762  a
Q763  a
Q764  b
Q765  d
Q766  b

# Documents

## Q767

To drive on the road learners MUST

*Mark one answer*

- a   have NO penalty points on their licence
- b   have taken professional instruction
- c   have a signed, valid provisional licence
- d   apply for a driving test within 12 months

## Q768

To supervise a learner driver you must

*Mark two answers*

- a   have held a full licence for at least 3 years
- b   be at least 21
- c   be an approved driving instructor
- d   hold an advanced driving certificate

## Q769

Your driving licence must be signed by

*Mark one answer*

- a   a police officer
- b   a driving instructor
- c   your next of kin
- d   yourself

## Q770

What is the legal minimum insurance cover you must have to drive on public roads?

*Mark one answer*

- a   Third party, fire and theft
- b   Fully comprehensive
- c   Third party only
- d   Personal injury cover

## Q771

For which TWO of these must you show your motor insurance certificate?

*Mark two answers*

- a   When you are taking your driving test
- b   When buying or selling a vehicle
- c   When a police officer asks you for it
- d   When you are taxing your vehicle
- e   When having an MOT inspection

## Q772

Vehicle excise duty is often called 'Road Tax' or 'The Tax Disc'. You must

*Mark one answer*

- a   keep it with your registration document
- b   display it clearly on your vehicle
- c   keep it concealed safely in your vehicle
- d   carry it on you at all times

## Q773

A police officer asks to see your driving documents. You do not have them with you. You may produce them at a police station within

*Mark one answer*

- a   five days
- b   seven days
- c   14 days
- d   21 days

**Q774**

Before driving anyone else's motor vehicle you should make sure that

*Mark one answer*
- a the vehicle owner has third party insurance cover
- b your own vehicle has insurance cover
- c the vehicle is insured for your use
- d the owner has left the insurance documents in the vehicle

**Q775**

Your car has third party insurance. What does this cover?

*Mark three answers*
- a Damage to your own car
- b Damage to your car by fire
- c Injury to another person
- d Damage to someone's property
- e Damage to other vehicles
- f Injury to yourself

**Q776**

The cost of your insurance may be reduced if

*Mark one answer*
- a your car is large and powerful
- b you are using the car for work purposes
- c you have penalty points on your licence
- d you are over 25 years old

**Q777**

Motor cars and motorcycles must FIRST have an MOT test certificate when they are

*Mark one answer*
- a one year old
- b three years old
- c five years old
- d seven years old

**Q778**

An MOT certificate is normally valid for

*Mark one answer*
- a three years after the date it was issued
- b 10,000 miles
- c one year after the date it was issued
- d 30,000 miles

**Q779**

Your car needs an MOT certificate. If you drive without one this could invalidate your

*Mark one answer*
- a vehicle service record
- b insurance
- c road tax disc
- d vehicle registration document

## Q780

When is it legal to drive a car over three years old without an MOT certificate?

*Mark one answer*

- a Up to seven days after the old certificate has run out
- b When driving to an MOT centre to arrange an appointment
- c Just after buying a secondhand car with no MOT
- d When driving to an appointment at an MOT centre

## Q781

Your vehicle needs a current MOT certificate. You do not have one. Until you do have one you will not be able to renew your

*Mark one answer*

- a driving licence
- b vehicle insurance
- c road tax disc
- d vehicle registration document

## Q782

Which of these vehicles is NOT required to have an MOT certificate?

*Mark two answers*

- a Police vehicle
- b Small trailer
- c Ambulance
- d Caravan

## Q783

Which THREE of the following do you need before you can drive legally?

*Mark three answers*

- a A valid signed driving licence
- b A valid tax disc displayed on your vehicle
- c Proof of your identity
- d Proper insurance cover
- e Breakdown cover
- f A vehicle handbook

## Q784

Which THREE pieces of information are found on a vehicle registration document?

*Mark three answers*

- a Registered keeper
- b Make of the vehicle
- c Service history details
- d Date of the MOT
- e Type of insurance cover
- f Engine size

## Q785

You have a duty to contact the licensing authority when

*Mark three answers*

- a you go abroad on holiday
- b you change your vehicle
- c you change your name
- d your job status is changed
- e your permanent address changes
- f your job involves travelling abroad

## Q786

You must notify the licensing authority when

*Mark three answers*

- ○ a   your health affects your driving
- ○ b   your eyesight does not meet a set standard
- ○ c   you intend lending your vehicle
- ○ d   your vehicle requires an MOT certificate
- ○ e   you change your vehicle

## Q787

You have just bought a secondhand vehicle. When should you tell the licensing authority of change of ownership?

*Mark one answer*

- ○ a   Immediately
- ○ b   After 28 days
- ○ c   When an MOT is due
- ○ d   Only when you insure it

## Answers and Explanations

Q767   **c**   You are not allowed to drive until you have applied for and received your provisional licence and have signed it in ink.

Q768   **a, b**

Q769   **d**   Your driving licence is not valid until you have signed it in ink.

Q770   **c**   This only covers damage to other people and their property.

Q771   **c, d**

Q772   **b**

Q773   **b**   You may select the police station of your choice.

Q774   **c**   Your own vehicle insurance may cover you as a passenger in another person's vehicle but very rarely covers you to drive it.

Q775   **c, d, e**

Q776   **d**   Drivers over 25 years old have less accidents than younger drivers. As they make fewer insurance claims, the cost of their premiums is usually less.

Q777   **b**

Q778   **c**

Q779   **b**

Q780   **d**   If your car is over three years old and has no valid MOT certificate, you must pre-book an appointment at an MOT centre before you drive it there.

Q781   **c**   When you renew your road tax disc you must produce a valid certificate of insurance and also a current MOT certificate if your car is over three years old.

Q782   **b, d**

Q783   **a, b, d**

Q784   **a, b, f**

Q785   **b, c, e**

Q786   **a, b, e**

Q787   **a**

**Driving Theory Test Questions**

# Accident Handling

### Q788

Which of these items should you carry in your vehicle for use in the event of an accident?

*Mark three answers*
- a  Road map
- b  Can of petrol
- c  Jump leads
- d  Fire extinguisher
- e  First Aid kit
- f  Warning triangle

### Q789

At the scene of an accident you should

*Mark one answer*
- a  not put yourself at risk
- b  go to those casualties who are screaming
- c  pull everybody out of their vehicles
- d  leave vehicle engines switched on

### Q790

You are the first to arrive at the scene of an accident. Which FOUR of these should you do?

*Mark four answers*
- a  Leave as soon as another motorist arrives
- b  Switch off the vehicle engine(s)
- c  Move uninjured people away from the vehicle(s)
- d  Call the emergency services
- e  Warn other traffic

### Q791

An accident has just happened. An injured person is lying in the busy road. What is the FIRST thing you should do to help?

*Mark one answer*
- a  Treat the person for shock
- b  Warn other traffic
- c  Place them in the recovery position
- d  Make sure the injured person is kept warm

### Q792

You are the first person to arrive at an accident where people are badly injured. Which THREE should you do?

*Mark three answers*
- a  Switch on your own hazard warning lights
- b  Make sure that someone telephones for an ambulance
- c  Try and get people who are injured to drink something
- d  Move the people who are injured clear of their vehicles
- e  Get people who are not injured clear of the scene

### Q793

You arrive at an accident. A motorcyclist is unconscious. Your FIRST priority is the casualty's

*Mark one answer*
- a  breathing
- b  bleeding
- c  broken bones
- d  bruising

**Q794**

You arrive at the scene of a motorcycle accident. The rider is injured. When should the helmet be removed?

*Mark one answer*

- a Only when it is essential
- b Always straight away
- c Only when the motorcyclist asks
- d Always, unless they are in shock

**Q795**

You arrive at a serious motorcycle accident. The motorcyclist is unconscious and bleeding. Your main priorities should be to

*Mark three answers*

- a try to stop the bleeding
- b make a list of witnesses
- c check the casualty's breathing
- d take the numbers of the vehicles involved
- e sweep up any loose debris
- f check the casualty's airways

**Q796**

At an accident a casualty is unconscious. Which THREE of the following should you check urgently?

*Mark three answers*

- a Circulation
- b Airway
- c Shock
- d Breathing
- e Broken bones

**Q797**

In first aid what does ABC stand for?

*Mark three answers*

- a Airway
- b Bleeding
- c Conscious
- d Breathing
- e Circulation
- f Alert

**Q798**

You arrive at the scene of an accident. It has just happened and someone is unconscious. Which of the following should be given urgent priority to help them?

*Mark three answers*

- a Clear the airway and keep it open
- b Try to get them to drink water
- c Check that they are breathing
- d Look for any witnesses
- e Stop any heavy bleeding
- f Take the numbers of vehicles involved

**Q799**

At an accident someone is unconscious. Your main priorities should be to

*Mark three answers*
- ○ a   sweep up the broken glass
- ○ b   take the names of witnesses
- ○ c   count the number of vehicles involved
- ○ d   check the airway is clear
- ○ e   make sure they are breathing
- ○ f   stop any heavy bleeding

**Q800**

You have stopped at the scene of an accident to give help. Which THREE things should you do?

*Mark three answers*
- ○ a   Keep injured people warm and comfortable
- ○ b   Keep injured people calm by talking to them reassuringly
- ○ c   Keep injured people on the move by walking them around
- ○ d   Give injured people a warm drink
- ○ e   Make sure that injured people are not left alone

**Q801**

At an accident a small child is not breathing. When giving mouth to mouth you should breathe

*Mark one answer*
- ○ a   sharply
- ○ b   gently
- ○ c   heavily
- ○ d   rapidly

**Q802**

You arrive at the scene of an accident. It has just happened and someone is injured. Which of the following should be given urgent priority?

*Mark three answers*
- ○ a   Stop any severe bleeding
- ○ b   Get them a warm drink
- ○ c   Check that their breathing is OK
- ○ d   Take numbers of vehicles involved
- ○ e   Look for witnesses
- ○ f   Clear their airway and keep it open

**Q803**

At an accident a casualty has stopped breathing. You should

*Mark two answers*
- ○ a   remove anything that is blocking the mouth
- ○ b   keep the head tilted forwards as far as possible
- ○ c   raise the legs to help with circulation
- ○ d   try to give the casualty something to drink
- ○ e   keep the head tilted back as far as possible

**Q804**

There has been an accident. The driver is suffering from shock. You should

*Mark two answers*
- ○ a   give them a drink
- ○ b   reassure them
- ○ c   not leave them alone
- ○ d   offer them a cigarette
- ○ e   ask who caused the accident

## Q805

You are at the scene of an accident. Someone is suffering from shock. You should

*Mark four answers*

○ a   reassure them constantly
○ b   offer them a cigarette
○ c   keep them warm
○ d   avoid moving them if possible
○ e   loosen any tight clothing
○ f   give them a warm drink

## Q806

Which of the following should you NOT do at the scene of an accident?

*Mark one answer*

○ a   Warn other traffic by switching on your hazard warning lights
○ b   Call the emergency services immediately
○ c   Offer someone a cigarette to calm them down
○ d   Ask drivers to switch off their engines

## Q807

You are at the scene of an accident. Someone is suffering from shock. You should

*Mark three answers*

○ a   offer them a cigarette
○ b   offer them a warm drink
○ c   keep them warm
○ d   loosen any tight clothing
○ e   reassure them constantly

## Q808

You have to treat someone for shock at the scene of an accident. You should

*Mark one answer*

○ a   reassure them constantly
○ b   walk them around to calm them down
○ c   give them something cold to drink
○ d   cool them down as soon as possible

## Q809

You arrive at the scene of a motorcycle accident. No other vehicle is involved. The rider is unconscious, lying in the middle of the road. The first thing you should do is

*Mark one answer*

○ a   move the rider out of the road
○ b   warn other traffic
○ c   clear the road of debris
○ d   give the rider reassurance

## Q810

To start mouth to mouth on a casualty you should

*Mark three answers*

○ a   tilt their head forward
○ b   clear the airway
○ c   turn them on their side
○ d   tilt their head back
○ e   pinch the nostrils together
○ f   put their arms across their chest

## Q811

When you are giving mouth to mouth you should only stop when

*Mark one answer*

- a    you think the casualty is dead
- b    the casualty can breathe without help
- c    the casualty has turned blue
- d    you think the ambulance is coming

## Q812

You arrive at the scene of an accident. There has been an engine fire and someone's hands and arms have been burnt. You should NOT

*Mark one answer*

- a    douse the burn thoroughly with cool liquid
- b    lay the casualty down
- c    remove anything sticking to the burn
- d    reassure them constantly

## Q813

You arrive at an accident where someone is suffering from severe burns. You should

*Mark one answer*

- a    apply lotions to the injury
- b    burst any blisters
- c    remove anything stuck to the burns
- d    douse the burns with cool liquid

## Q814

You arrive at an accident where someone is suffering from severe burns. You should

*Mark one answer*

- a    burst any blisters
- b    douse the burns thoroughly with cool liquid
- c    apply lotions to the injury
- d    remove anything sticking to the burns

## Q815

You arrive at the scene of an accident. A pedestrian has a severe bleeding wound on their leg, although it is not broken. What should you do?

*Mark two answers*

- a    Dab the wound to stop bleeding
- b    Keep both legs flat on the ground
- c    Apply firm pressure to the wound
- d    Raise the leg to lessen bleeding
- e    Fetch them a warm drink

## Q816

You arrive at the scene of an accident. A passenger is bleeding badly from an arm wound. What should you do?

*Mark one answer*

- a    Apply pressure over the wound and keep the arm down
- b    Dab the wound
- c    Get them a drink
- d    Apply pressure over the wound and raise the arm

**Q817**

You arrive at the scene of an accident. A pedestrian is bleeding heavily from a leg wound but the leg is not broken. What should you do?

*Mark one answer*

○ a  Dab the wound to stop the bleeding
○ b  Keep both legs flat on the ground
○ c  Apply firm pressure to the wound
○ d  Fetch them a warm drink

**Q818**

At an accident a casualty is unconscious but still breathing. You should only move them if

*Mark one answer*

○ a  an ambulance is on its way
○ b  bystanders advise you to
○ c  there is further danger
○ d  bystanders will help you to

**Q819**

At an accident you suspect a casualty has back injuries. The area is safe. You should

*Mark one answer*

○ a  offer them a drink
○ b  not move them
○ c  raise their legs
○ d  offer them a cigarette

**Q820**

At an accident it is important to look after the casualty. When the area is safe, you should

*Mark one answer*
○ a  get them out of the vehicle
○ b  give them a drink
○ c  give them something to eat
○ d  keep them in the vehicle

**Q821**

A tanker is involved in an accident. Which sign would show that the tanker is carrying dangerous goods?

*Mark one answer*
○ a

○ b

○ c

○ d

## Q822

While driving, a warning light on your vehicle's instrument panel comes on. You should

*Mark one answer*

- a   continue if the engine sounds alright
- b   hope that it is just a temporary electrical fault
- c   deal with the problem when there is more time
- d   check out the problem quickly and safely

## Q823

For which TWO should you use hazard warning lights?

*Mark two answers*

- a   When you slow down quickly on a motorway because of a hazard ahead
- b   When you have broken down
- c   When you wish to stop on double yellow lines
- d   When you need to park on the pavement

## Q824

For which THREE should you use your hazard warning lights?

*Mark three answers*

- a   When you are parking in a restricted area
- b   When you are temporarily obstructing traffic
- c   To warn following traffic of a hazard ahead
- d   When you have broken down
- e   When only stopping for a short time

## Q825

When are you allowed to use hazard warning lights?

*Mark one answer*

- a   When stopped and temporarily obstructing traffic
- b   When driving during darkness without headlights
- c   When parked for shopping on double yellow lines
- d   When travelling slowly because you are lost

## Q826

When should you switch on your hazard warning lights?

*Mark one answer*

- a   When you cannot avoid causing an obstruction
- b   When you are driving slowly due to bad weather
- c   When you are towing a broken down vehicle
- d   When you are parked on double yellow lines

## Q827

You are in an accident on a two-way road. You have a warning triangle with you. At what distance before the obstruction should you place the warning triangle?

*Mark one answer*

- a   25 metres (82 feet)
- b   45 metres (147 feet)
- c   100 metres (328 feet)
- d   150 metres (492 feet)

### Q828

You have broken down on a two-way road. You have a warning triangle. You should place the warning triangle at least how far from your vehicle?

*Mark one answer*

- a   5 metres (16 feet)
- b   25 metres (82 feet)
- c   45 metres (147 feet)
- d   100 metres (328 feet)

### Q829

The police may ask you to produce which three of these documents following an accident?

*Mark three answers*

- a   Vehicle registration document
- b   Driving licence
- c   Theory test certificate
- d   Insurance certificate
- e   MOT test certificate
- f   Road tax disc

### Q830

You have broken down on a two-way road. You have a warning triangle. It should be displayed

*Mark one answer*

- a   on the roof of your vehicle
- b   at least 150 metres (492 feet) behind your vehicle
- c   at least 45 metres (147 feet) behind your vehicle
- d   just behind your vehicle

### Q831

You are involved in an accident with another driver. Someone is injured. Your vehicle is damaged. Which FOUR of the following should you find out?

*Mark four answers*

- a   Whether the driver owns the other vehicle involved
- b   The other driver's name, address and telephone number
- c   The car make and registration number of the other vehicle
- d   The occupation of the other driver
- e   The details of the other driver's vehicle insurance
- f   Whether the other driver is licensed to drive

## Q832

You have an accident while driving and someone is injured. You do not produce your insurance certificate at the time. You must report it to the police as soon as possible, or in any case within

*Mark one answer*

- a  24 hours
- b  48 hours
- c  five days
- d  seven days

## Q833

At a railway level crossing the red light signal continues to flash after a train has gone by. What should you do?

KEEP
CROSSING
CLEAR

*Mark one answer*

- a  Phone the signal operator
- b  Alert drivers behind you
- c  Wait
- d  Proceed with caution

## Q834

You break down on a level crossing. The lights have not yet begun to flash. Which THREE things should you do?

*Mark three answers*

- a  Telephone the signal operator
- b  Leave your vehicle and get everyone clear
- c  Walk down the track and signal the next train
- d  Move the vehicle if a signal operator tells you to
- e  Tell drivers behind what has happened

## Q835

You have stalled in the middle of a level crossing and cannot restart the engine. The warning bell starts to ring. You should

*Mark one answer*

- a  get out and clear of the crossing
- b  run down the track to warn the signal operator
- c  carry on trying to restart the engine
- d  push the vehicle clear of the crossing

## Q836

You see a car on the hard shoulder of a motorway with a HELP pennant displayed. This means the driver is most likely to be

*Mark one answer*

- a  a disabled person
- b  first aid trained
- c  a foreign visitor
- d  a rescue patrol person

Q837

Your vehicle has broken down on an automatic railway level crossing. What should you do FIRST?

*Mark one answer*

○ a  Get everyone out of the vehicle and clear of the crossing
○ b  Phone the signal operator so that trains can be stopped
○ c  Walk along the track to give warning to any approaching trains
○ d  Try to push the vehicle clear of the crossing as soon as possible

Q838

Your tyre bursts while you are driving. Which TWO things should you do?

*Mark two answers*

○ a  Pull on the handbrake
○ b  Brake as quickly as possible
○ c  Pull up slowly at the side of the road
○ d  Hold the steering wheel firmly to keep control
○ e  Continue on at a normal speed

Q839

Which TWO things should you do when a front tyre bursts?

*Mark two answers*

○ a  Apply the handbrake to stop the vehicle
○ b  Brake firmly and quickly
○ c  Let the vehicle roll to a stop
○ d  Hold the steering wheel lightly
○ e  Grip the steering wheel firmly

Q840

You are driving on the motorway and get a puncture. You should

*Mark one answer*

○ a  pull onto the hard shoulder as safely as possible
○ b  stop in the lane you are in and change the wheel
○ c  pull into the central reservation as safely as possible
○ d  stop in any lane but use emergency flashers

Q841

Your vehicle has a puncture on a motorway. What should you do?

*Mark one answer*

○ a  Drive slowly to the next service area to get assistance
○ b  Pull up on the hard shoulder. Change the wheel as quickly as possible
○ c  Pull up on the hard shoulder. Use the emergency phone to get assistance
○ d  Switch on your hazard lights. Stop in your lane

Q842

On the motorway the hard shoulder should be used

*Mark one answer*

○ a  to answer a mobile phone
○ b  when an emergency arises
○ c  for a short rest when tired
○ d  to check a road atlas

### Q843

What TWO safeguards could you take against fire risk to your vehicle?

*Mark two answers*

- a  Keep water levels above maximum
- b  Carry a fire extinguisher
- c  Avoid driving with a full tank of petrol
- d  Use unleaded petrol
- e  Check out any strong smell of petrol
- f  Use low octane fuel

### Q844

You have broken down on a motorway. When you use the emergency telephone you will be asked

*Mark three answers*

- a  for the number on the telephone that you are using
- b  for your driving licence details
- c  for the name of your vehicle insurance company
- d  for details of yourself and your vehicle
- e  whether you belong to a motoring organisation

### Q845

An injured motorcyclist is lying unconscious in the road. You should

*Mark one answer*

- a  remove the safety helmet
- b  seek medical assistance
- c  move the person off the road
- d  remove the leather jacket

### Q846

You are on the motorway. Luggage falls from your vehicle. What should you do?

*Mark one answer*

- a  Stop at the next emergency telephone and contact the police
- b  Stop on the motorway and put on hazard lights whilst you pick it up
- c  Reverse back up the motorway to pick it up
- d  Pull up on the hard shoulder and wave traffic down

### Q847

You are travelling on a motorway. A suitcase falls from your vehicle. There are valuables in the suitcase. What should you do?

*Mark one answer*

- a  Reverse your vehicle carefully and collect the case as quickly as possible
- b  Stop wherever you are and pick up the case but only when there is a safe gap
- c  Stop on the hard shoulder and use the emergency telephone to inform the police
- d  Stop on the hard shoulder and then retrieve the suitcase yourself

### Q848

You are driving on a motorway. A large box falls onto the carriageway from a lorry ahead of you. The lorry does not stop. You should

*Mark one answer*

○ a   drive to the next emergency telephone and inform the police

○ b   catch up with the lorry and try to get the driver's attention

○ c   stop close to the box and switch on your hazard warning lights until the police arrive

○ d   pull over to the hard shoulder, then try and remove the box

### Q849

You are driving on a motorway. When can you use hazard warning lights?

*Mark two answers*

○ a   When a vehicle is following too closely

○ b   When you slow down quickly because of danger ahead

○ c   When you are towing another vehicle

○ d   When driving on the hard shoulder

○ e   When you have broken down on the hard shoulder

## Answers and Explanations

Q788   d, e, f

Q789   a

Q790   b, c, d, e

Q791   b   Warning other traffic first helps stop the accident getting even worse.

Q792   a, b, e

Q793   a

Q794   a

Q795   a, c, f   Injuries should be dealt with in the order Airway, Breathing then Circulation and bleeding.

Q796   a, b, d

Q797   a, d, e

Q798   a, c, e   Note that these are the things to which you should give urgent priority.

Q799   d, e, f

Q800   a, b, e   You should not move injured people unless they are in danger; nor should you give them anything to drink.

Q801   b

Q802   a, c, f

Q803   a, e

Q804   b, c

Q805   a, c, d, e

Q806   c

Q807   c, d, e

Q808   a

Q809   b   Note that this is the FIRST thing to do. By warning other traffic you help reduce the risk of more collisions.

Q810   b, d, e

Q811   b

Q812   c

Q813   d

Q814   b

Q815   c, d
Q816   d
Q817   c
Q818   c
Q819   b   If you move the casualty you may worsen their injury.
Q820   d
Q821   b
Q822   d
Q823   a, b
Q824   b, c, d
Q825   a
Q826   a
Q827   b
Q828   c   45 metres is recommended on two-way roads and 150 metres on motorways and dual carriageways.
Q829   b, d, e
Q830   c
Q831   a, b, c, e
Q832   a   Note that you have 24 hours in which to report the accident but are allowed up to seven days in which to produce your driving licence, insurance and MOT certificates if required to do so.
Q833   c   This usually means another train is coming.
Q834   a, b, d
Q835   a   A train may arrive within seconds so 'a' is the only safe possibility.
Q836   a
Q837   a   Your first action is to get everyone to safety.
Q838   c, d   You will need both hands firmly on the wheel in order to control the car, and using the gears or brakes is likely to make your car swerve. When possible, it is safest just to let your car roll to a halt at the side of the road.

Q839   c, e
Q840   a
Q841   c   The hard shoulder of a motorway is a dangerous place and 'c' is the safest course of action. It can be particularly dangerous to try to change an offside wheel as you may be very close to fast-moving traffic in the left-hand lane.
Q842   b
Q843   b, e
Q844   a, d, e
Q845   b
Q846   a
Q847   c
Q848   a
Q849   b, e

**Driving Theory Test Questions**

# Vehicle Loading

## Q850

Overloading your vehicle can seriously affect the

*Mark two answers*
- a   gearbox
- b   steering
- c   handling
- d   battery life
- e   journey time

## Q851

Who is responsible for making sure that a vehicle is not overloaded?

*Mark one answer*
- a   The driver or rider of the vehicle
- b   The owner of the items being carried
- c   The person who loaded the vehicle
- d   The owner of the vehicle

## Q852

On which TWO occasions might you inflate your tyres to more than the recommended normal pressure?

*Mark two answers*
- a   When the roads are slippery
- b   When driving fast for a long distance
- c   When the tyre tread is worn below 2mm
- d   When carrying a heavy load
- e   When the weather is cold
- f   When the vehicle is fitted with anti-lock brakes

## Q853

Any load that is carried on a roof rack MUST be

*Mark one answer*
- a   securely fastened when driving
- b   carried only when strictly necessary
- c   as light as possible
- d   covered with plastic sheeting

## Q854

A heavy load on your roof rack will

*Mark one answer*
- a   improve the road holding
- b   reduce the stopping distance
- c   make the steering lighter
- d   reduce stability

## Q855

You should load a trailer so that the weight is

*Mark one answer*
- a   mostly over the nearside wheel
- b   evenly distributed
- c   mainly at the front
- d   mostly at the rear

## Q856

Your vehicle is fitted with child safety door locks. You should use these so that children inside the car cannot open

*Mark one answer*
- a   the right-hand doors
- b   the left-hand doors
- c   the rear doors
- d   any of the doors

## Q857

What do child locks in a vehicle do?

*Mark one answer*
- a Lock the seat belt buckles in place
- b Lock the rear windows in the up position
- c Stop children from opening rear doors
- d Stop the rear seats from tipping forward

## Q858

Which THREE are suitable restraints for a child under three years?

*Mark three answers*
- a A child seat
- b An adult holding a child
- c An adult seat belt
- d A lap belt
- e A harness
- f A baby carrier

## Q859

You are planning to tow a caravan. Which of these will mostly help to aid the vehicle handling?

*Mark one answer*
- a A jockey-wheel fitted to the towbar
- b Power steering fitted to the towing vehicle
- c Anti-lock brakes fitted to the towing vehicle
- d A stabiliser fitted to the towbar

## Q860

Before towing a caravan you should ensure that heavy items in it are loaded

*Mark one answer*
- a as high as possible, mainly over the axle(s)
- b as low as possible, mainly over the axle(s)
- c as low as possible, forward of the axle(s)
- d as high as possible, forward of the axle(s)

## Q861

A trailer must stay securely hitched-up to the towing vehicle. What additional safety device can be fitted to the trailer braking system?

*Mark one answer*
- a Stabiliser
- b Jockey wheel
- c Corner steadies
- d Breakaway cable

## Q862

If a trailer swerves or snakes when you are towing it you should

*Mark one answer*
- a ease off the accelerator and reduce your speed
- b let go of the steering wheel and let it correct itself
- c brake hard and hold the pedal down
- d increase your speed as quickly as possible

## Q863

Are passengers allowed to ride in a caravan that is being towed?

*Mark one answer*

- a  Yes
- b  No
- c  Only if all the seats in the towing vehicle are full
- d  Only if a stabilizer is fitted

## Q864

You are towing a caravan along a motorway. The caravan begins to swerve from side to side. What should you do?

*Mark one answer*

- a  Ease off the accelerator slowly
- b  Steer sharply from side to side
- c  Do an emergency stop
- d  Speed up a little

## Q865

How can you stop a caravan snaking from side to side?

*Mark one answer*

- a  Turn the steering wheel slowly to each side
- b  Accelerate to increase your speed
- c  Stop as quickly as you can
- d  Slow down very gradually

## Q866

You are towing a small trailer on a busy three-lane motorway. All the lanes are open. You must

*Mark two answers*

- a  not exceed 60 mph
- b  not overtake
- c  have a stabiliser fitted
- d  use only the left and centre lanes

---

### Answers and Explanations

Q850  **b, c**
Q851  **a**
Q852  **b, d**
Q853  **a**  The word 'MUST' in the question makes 'a' correct.
Q854  **d**  A heavy load on the roof will shift the centre of gravity of your vehicle and could make you more likely to skid or roll over.
Q855  **b**  This creates the greatest stability.
Q856  **c**
Q857  **c**  Child locks prevent the rear doors being opened from the inside.
Q858  **a, e, f**
Q859  **d**
Q860  **b**  This reduces the risk of the caravan swerving about or being top heavy and tipping over.
Q861  **d**
Q862  **a**  Options 'b', 'c' or 'd' would

all be likely to make the
problem worse.

Q863  b
Q864  a
Q865  d
Q866  a, d

## Driving Theory Test Questions

# Notes

# For information on learning to drive with a BSM instructor please contact your local BSM centre on:

# 0345 276 276

BSM instructors operate under a franchise with
The British School of Motoring Limited, the largest organisation of its kind
in the world.

The two additional books in the series, *Pass Your Driving Test* and *Pass Your Driving Theory Test*, are available from all BSM centres and from all good bookshops.